WOMEN OF THE BIBLE

New Testament

Rose Visual Bible Studies

Women of the Bible: New Testament
Rose Visual Bible Studies

Published by Rose Publishing
An imprint of Tyndale House Ministries
Carol Stream, Illinois
rose-publishing.com

ISBN 978-1-64938-028-9

Author: Cyndi Parker (PhD, University of Gloucestershire) teaches in seminaries, universities, and churches around the world. Cyndi is the Professor of Holy Land Studies at the Israel Bible Center and an adjunct professor at Jerusalem University College. She hosts the *Context Matters* podcast and publishes papers focused on the cultural and geographical context of the Bible. Cyndi lived in Jerusalem for five years, has led dozens of trips to Israel, and continues to develop innovative, educational trips that inspire students of all ages through experiential education.

Special thanks to Rachel Asproth, whose poem "A Prayer for Women: Remember Your Daughters" inspired the prayers in this study. This poem first appeared in the Summer 2017 issue of CBE's *Mutuality* magazine (www.cbeinternational.org).

Printed in China
March 2025, 2nd printing

Contents

MOTHERS OF JESUS
Tamar, Rahab, Ruth, Bathsheba, and Mary

Page 7

MARY OF NAZARETH
Student of Scripture

Page 25

ANNA
A Faithful Witness

Page 41

THE WOMAN AT THE WELL
Her Remarkable Encounter

Page 55

MARY AND MARTHA
Sisters of Devotion and Hospitality

Page 71

BUILDERS OF THE CHURCH
The Women of Romans 16

Page 83

LEADER'S GUIDE

Page 97

"Blessed is she who has believed that the Lord would fulfill his promises to her!"

Luke 1:45

Women of the New Testament

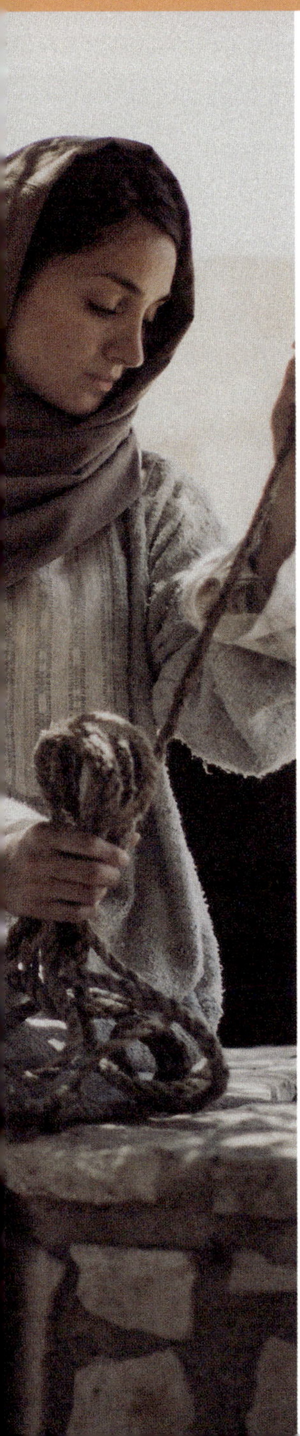

God has given us the fullness of his plan in both the Old and New Testaments—the Old forming the basis for the New, the New explaining the Old. The coming of Jesus Christ, detailed in the New Testament, fulfilled decrees of salvation and justice God had promised to his people centuries before. Not surprisingly, God appointed specific women to play significant roles in the story of Jesus' earthly life and the church that blossomed after him. Each of the women highlighted in this study has something to teach us about God. If we look closely enough, we may also notice how deeply God trusts his daughters to proclaim to *everyone* the good news of who he is and how he is at work in the world.

Women of the Bible: New Testament highlights the lives of several women you may or may not be familiar with. We start with the women listed in Jesus' genealogy: Who were they, and how did they merit inclusion in a typically male-only list? The second session is dedicated to Mary, the mother of Jesus. She is one of the few women we can follow through the entirety of Jesus' life, and here we will focus on her as a student of Scripture. Next, we'll learn about Anna, whose lifelong faith in God's promises to send a Savior spills over into one of the first recorded evangelistic outreaches. The following two sessions turn familiar passages on their heads, prompting us to reexamine the assumptions modern audiences bring to the story of Martha and Mary and the story of the Samaritan woman at the well. We end with Paul and his shout-out in Romans 16 to many of the people who had partnered with him in ministry. It's time for a fresh look at the strategic women mentioned in Paul's list!

Perhaps you've read these narratives before but have never discovered how history, culture, and geography flavor their background. In the following sessions, you'll study aspects of these stories that aren't commonly discussed but will better inform your perspective and broaden your understanding of the original intent behind their inclusion in the Bible. Although in several ways these women's lives differed from ours today, we also see our own hopes and challenges reflected in how they've overcome obstacles and persevered in believing God's promises. In short, they relied on the same God we know and worship, and he blessed them as he blesses us. Are you ready to discover new and interesting insights into key women of the New Testament? Bring your curiosity as you learn more about the God of the Bible and your own transformative role in the story God is writing.

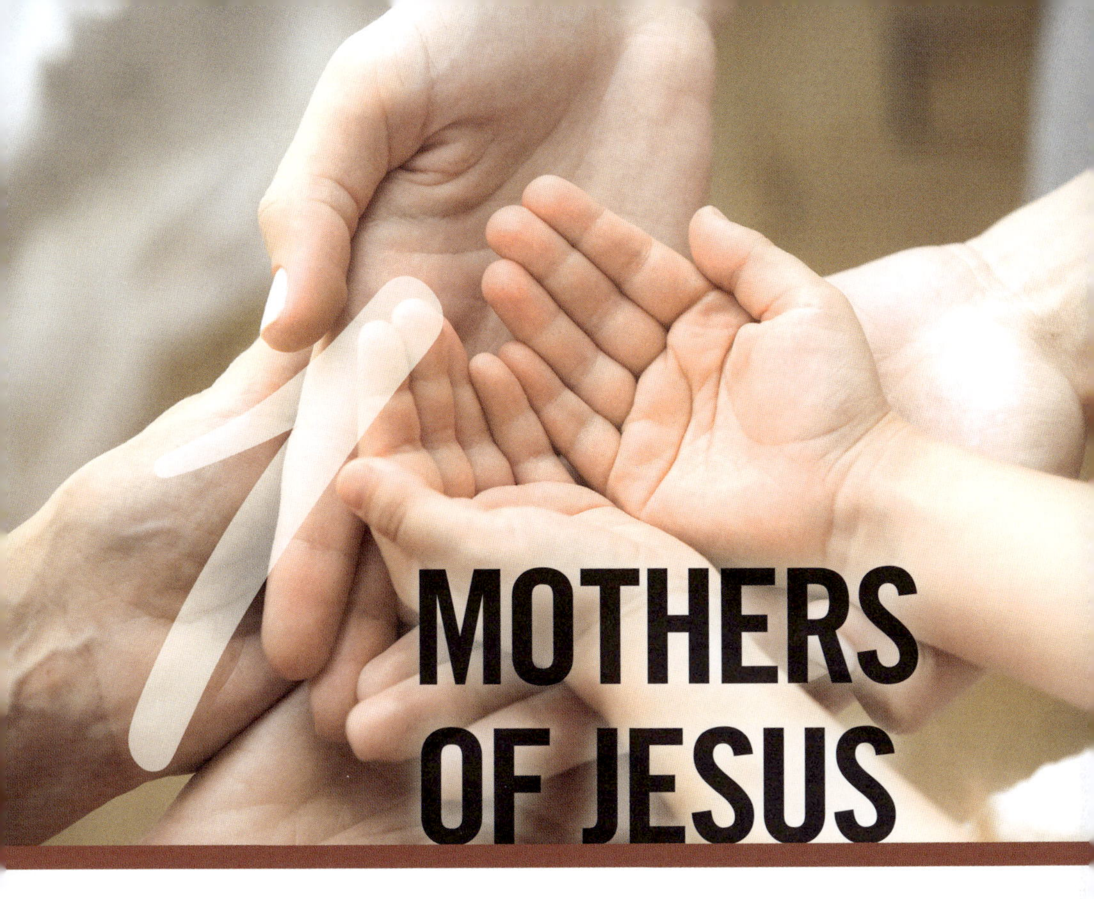

MOTHERS OF JESUS

Tamar, Rahab, Ruth, Bathsheba, and Mary

Mothers of Jesus

Tracing family history has become a pastime for some people. These days, chances are pretty high you've noticed the popularity of DNA testing to discover your ancestry, and connecting the dots through genealogy websites has also become more common. But western society traditionally has not made a huge effort to trace family roots or understand personal identity based on a long list of ancestors. Even today we're more likely to think of ourselves as individuals with a future that doesn't depend on our background.

The world of the New Testament, however, was completely different. People not only valued the stories of their ancestors but also understood their personal identity based on connections to the past. In fact, connection was so important that Matthew opens his gospel with a list of the radical people who made up Jesus' family tree. Each name demonstrates that Jesus' life was connected to the larger Israelite storyline and stirs up readers' anticipation for the grandness of who Jesus would become. Interestingly, Matthew's genealogy breaks the traditional mold by specifically identifying women. To answer why, let's dig into their fascinating stories.

Read It

Key Bible Passage

For this session, read Matthew 1:1–17.

Optional Reading

Background stories of the women in Matthew's genealogy of Jesus:

- Tamar—Genesis 38
- Rahab—Joshua 2; 6
- Ruth—Ruth 1–4
- The wife of Uriah (Bathsheba)—2 Samuel 11
- Mary—Matthew 1:18–25

The optional reading offers insight into the women in Matthew's genealogy and helps us understand the background and path that led them to become mothers of Jesus.

"Jacob was the father of Joseph, the husband of Mary. Mary gave birth to Jesus, who is called the Messiah."

MATTHEW 1:16 NLT

Know It

1. When you read the Bible and come upon lists of names like the one in Matthew 1, do you think about why those specific names are there, or do you tend to skip over or skim the list and not think much about it?

2. In verse 1, Matthew tells us what the purpose is for his list of names and calls out that Jesus is the son of David, who is the son of Abraham. Why do you think Matthew set up his genealogy by anchoring it in these two Israelite patriarchs? (Hint: What stories or characteristics do you associate with both Abraham and David?)

3. Tamar, Rahab, Ruth, the wife of Uriah (Bathsheba), and Mary are the women identified in Matthew 1:1–17. What do you know about each of them beyond their mention in this genealogy?

Culture

During the time of Jesus, people valued their communities and families more than individual roles. They knew they had arrived at their situation in life because of those who had come before them. Children were taught to avoid bringing shame to the family's reputation, and wealth and place within the social hierarchy held more sway over a person's options than gender did. Women of high status enjoyed more freedom than men of low status.

The culture was also organized around a *patriarchal* structure defined by the father of the house. It was often *patrilocal* as well: A bride moved into her husband's house with his extended family, forming a *patrilineal* society where family lineage, and therefore family inheritance, was traced through the males—often the oldest son.

Such an arrangement explains why genealogies in the Bible usually record only male names. And although a long list of names might seem like a tedious read, each was significant to the writer and original readers and represented a moment in Israel's history. Genealogies in Scripture are like little packets of information strung together to create a narrative of a family's history with God.

Matthew's genealogy is no different. There is more here than meets the eye. He chose to mention people who didn't have admirable social standing, and he rejected the traditional method of documenting lineage only through firstborn sons. Even more shocking is that he adds women, and they are not the traditionally honored matriarchs! Matthew must be making an emphatic point by going off-script.

GENEALOGY OF JESUS,
the Son of David, the son of Abraham

1. **ABRAHAM**

2. Isaac

3. Jacob

4. Judah and ***Tamar***

5. Perez

6. Hezron

7. Ram

8. Amminadab

9. Nahshon

10. Salmon and ***Rahab***

11. Boaz and ***Ruth***

12. Obed

13. Jesse

14. **KING DAVID**

1. **KING DAVID** and ***the wife of Uriah***

2. Solomon

3. Rehoboam

4. Abijah

5. Asa

6. Jehoshaphat

7 Jehoram

8. Uzziah

9. Jotham

10. Ahaz

11. Hezekiah

12. Manasseh

13. Amon

14. Josiah

BABYLONIAN EXILE

1. Jeconiah

2. Shealtiel

3. Zerubbabel

4. Abihud

5. Eliakim

6. Azor

7. Zadok

8. Akim

9. Elihud

10. Eleazar

11. Matthan

12. Jacob

13. Joseph and ***Mary***

14. **JESUS, the Messiah**

Narrative

Matthew's gospel begins with a provocative introductory statement: Jesus is the Messiah—the son of David, who is the son of Abraham. Mentioning David and Abraham together creates a link between the long-cherished images of the ideal Israelite king (David) and the nation's patriarch (Abraham). Matthew follows that statement with a "stylized" genealogy to support his point. "Stylized" means he skipped over certain generations, but it does not mean his genealogy is false! Ancient writers had the freedom to stylize to prove their overall point. Matthew is persuasively telling readers to pay close attention to who Jesus is. In this session, we'll focus on the women in Matthew's list by learning their backstories.

Tamar (v. 3)

Tamar's story (Gen. 38) begins with Judah, one of Abraham's great-grandsons. Judah's oldest son, Er, married Tamar, but Er died before Tamar could have children. In such cases, it was common for a brother of the deceased husband to assume responsibility for the widow, including providing her with a child. Er's brother Onan was happy to sleep with Tamar, but he knew that if she became pregnant, the child would not be his. So he selfishly took measures to prevent her from becoming pregnant. Onan also died, and again Tamar was widowed without children. Judah should have taken responsibility for Tamar, but he dismissed her by telling her to wait and marry his youngest son.

Tamar decided to take matters into her own hands. She dressed as a prostitute and sat along the road, waiting for Judah to come along. Not knowing who she was, Judah had sex with her, and she became pregnant with twins. Her actions seem outrageous,

A Coded Message

Matthew lists fourteen generations from Abraham to David, another fourteen from David to the exile, and fourteen more from the exile to Jesus (Matt. 1:17). This division is organized around the high and low points of Israel's history. But what is the significance of the number fourteen? We need to understand that in ancient times, Hebrew letters were assigned numerical values. The first letter was 1, the second letter 2, etc. David's name has three letters (ד ו ד—d v d; Hebrew words back then contained consonants and no vowels). If we use the numbering code, ד is four and ו is six. The numbers in David's name (ד ו ד) add up to fourteen! Matthew is emphasizing (1) that Jesus belongs to the Israelite story that began with Abraham and continued through King David, and (2) that Jesus fulfills the prophecy of a Messiah who would descend from King David. Matthew's genealogy is a coded message designed to make readers sit up straight and pay attention to Jesus.

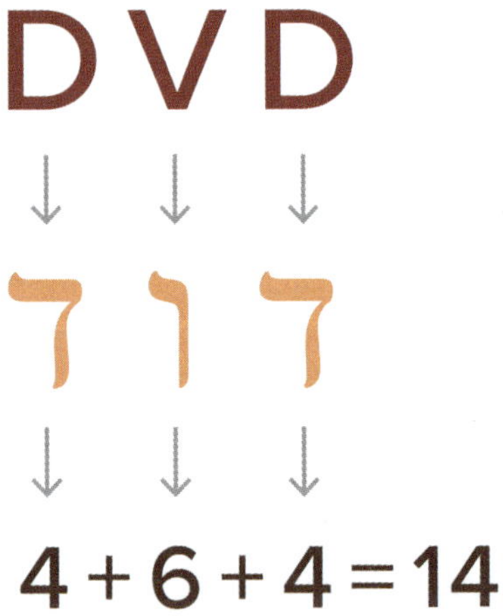

D V D

↓ ↓ ↓

ד ו ד

↓ ↓ ↓

4 + 6 + 4 = 14

David L. Turner in *Cornerstone Biblical Commentary*, vol. 11, offers this clarification: "The genealogy has three movements of fourteen generations: (1) from Abraham to David (1:2–6a), (2) from David to the Exile (1:6b–11), and (3) from the Exile to Jesus the Messiah (1:12–16). Careful readers will note that it is difficult to arrange the genealogy into three groups of fourteen generations, but Matthew was more interested in the symbolism of 'fourteen' than in the precision of his scheme" (Carol Stream, IL: Tyndale, 2005, 34).

but Tamar acted in a culturally appropriate way to seek justice. Please note, Tamar *dressed* like a prostitute—she did not become a prostitute! She ensured that Judah provided her with children and thus an inheritance. When Judah realized the magnitude of his mistake, he declared, "She is more righteous than I am" (v. 26). Tamar made a huge impact on the future Israelite nation. One of her twin sons, Perez, was an ancestor of King David (Ruth 4:18–22) and an important link in the birth of a Redeemer for Israel and the world.

Rahab (v. 5)

Rahab was a Canaanite prostitute who lived in the city of Jericho. When two Israelites were sent to spy out the land God had promised them, the spies stayed in Rahab's house to remain cloaked in secrecy (Josh. 2:1). The choice seems odd, but at that time the only place to remain unnoticed was in a house where people regularly came and went.

Rahab not only housed the spies but also hid them from Jericho's officials. She had heard about the wonders God did for the Israelites by rescuing them from Egypt and allowing them a safe journey. Rahab proclaimed to the spies, "The Lord your God is God in heaven above and on the earth below" (v. 11). She became the first Canaanite to declare the supremacy of the one true God.

Rahab asked the spies to protect her and her family when the Israelites attacked Jericho. The spies agreed, promising to spare anyone who found refuge in Rahab's house. What a remarkable story! Rahab saved her entire family because she recognized the power of Israel's God and boldly asked for mercy. According to Matthew, Rahab married an Israelite named Salmon and became a foremother of Boaz, which leads us to the next story.

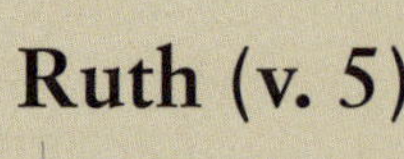

Ruth (v. 5)

Ruth's story begins in her future husband's hometown—Bethlehem in Israel. During a drought, a woman named Naomi, along with her family, moved east to the land of Moab with hopes of surviving there (Ruth 1:1). When Naomi's husband died, she was left with Mahlon and Kilion, her two sons. They eventually married Moabite women—Orpah and Ruth—but then Mahlon and Kilion died. Without a husband and children, Naomi's only hope was to return to Bethlehem so someone in her extended family could care for her. Along the way, Naomi encouraged Orpah and Ruth to return to their families so they could marry again. Orpah turned back, but Ruth stayed.

The residents in Bethlehem noticed Ruth's hard work and loyalty to Naomi. Ultimately, Boaz, one of Naomi's wealthy relatives, married Ruth, becoming the provider for both women. The book of Ruth concludes with its own genealogy, where we learn that Ruth and Boaz became the great-grandparents of King David.

Bathsheba, the Wife of Uriah (v. 6)

The next woman is described as "Uriah's wife," a title that refers to Bathsheba. Some translations add her name for clarity, but it isn't included in the Greek manuscripts. Bathsheba is called "the wife of Uriah" in 2 Samuel 11:3. King David had stayed in Jerusalem after sending his army to battle, and late one day he saw Bathsheba as he was walking on the roof of his palace. Notice that *he* was looking down at *her*. The Bible says she was “bathing” (v. 2), but that doesn’t mean she was soaking in a claw-foot tub.

In fact, bathing at that time was a matter of rubbing down with oil and scraping off impurities. It’s also possible Bathsheba was using a wet cloth to clean herself after completing her period (v. 4). Bathsheba was in the privacy of her home, but often this story is told as if she had purposely enticed David by soaking naked in a rooftop bubble bath. Such a scenario is not implied in the Bible! Rather, David lusted after Bathsheba while her husband, Uriah, was fighting David’s war.

David sent servants to bring Bathsheba to his palace, where it’s implied that David raped her. Bathsheba became pregnant, and David worried that if Uriah found out, he would seek retaliation. To protect himself, David crafted a way for Uriah to be killed in battle. After Bathsheba had mourned her husband’s death, David took her as his wife. Sadly, their son died soon after birth, but Bathsheba and David’s next son, Solomon, lived to become one of Israel’s great kings and an ancestor of Jesus.

Let’s circle back to the question of why Matthew called Bathsheba “Uriah’s wife” instead of “wife of David” or “mother of Solomon.” It’s possible his actions were a rebuke against David, or perhaps he intended to honor Uriah’s memory. Whatever the case, Bathsheba’s mention in Jesus’ genealogy reminds us that God can transform even the messiest of situations into a blessing for the entire world.

Mary, the Mother of Jesus (v. 16)

The final woman Matthew mentions is Mary, but we’ll save her story for the next session. Sufficient to notice here is that once more Matthew breaks a pattern. Joseph is called "the husband of Mary," a highly unusual way to refer to a man—in terms of his relationship to a woman. The genealogy states that "Mary was the mother of Jesus" but carefully leaves out a biological connection between Jesus and Joseph.

A Common Thread

Some suggest these women have a shady past in common, yet consider that Judah called Tamar "more righteous than I" in her quest for justice (Gen. 38:26). Rahab was identified as a prostitute, but her choices saved the spies from certain death and redeemed herself and her family. Ruth was praised for her strength of character. Bathsheba was violated, then suffered the death of her husband and first child. Those were not *her* bad choices in life. And Mary submitted to God's plan knowing others would accuse her of actions she had never taken.

Rather, *this* is the common thread: Social traditions do not constrict God. Ruth was a Moabite, Rahab a Canaanite—two nations that were Israel's enemies. Tamar and Bathsheba had suffered injustices. And Mary had a child in a most uncommon way! By including these women, Matthew highlights how God intervenes in history, through all kinds of people, to bring about his purposes. Matthew's lineage underscores God's faithfulness in the past and hints that it will continue through the birth of Jesus.

Live It

The genealogies sprinkled throughout the Bible show modern readers that family memories were honored and long-lasting. We may not know the names of fourteen generations of our ancestors, but the people living in Bible times did. What a great reminder that God's story reaches long before us and will continue long after us. As he writes his grand narrative, he still interacts kindly and mercifully with individuals, and he does not require that they represent a certain class or gender.

Life Application Questions

1. Do you notice particular patterns in the lives of your ancestors that match or differ from those in your own life? Can any of the blessings you enjoy today be traced back to God's work in their lives?

2. Choose one of these women and think about her story. What parts can you identify with? Do you recognize her story in the lives of anyone you know?

3. Because of Rahab's bold actions, her entire family was saved. How might Rahab's example inspire you to pray for the needs of your loved ones?

4. We could use descriptions like *immigrant*, *marginalized*, or *abused* for the women listed in Matthew 1, but those words would not tell their full story. Can you think of any labels we place on others that prevent us from seeing who they really are?

5. Have you ever felt like you didn't fit in with church crowds or were left out because you didn't match the Christian mold? Remember, God isn't restricted by our made-up cultural standards. How has God worked in your life despite your unconventional circumstances?

Prayer

God of our grandmothers,

God of all who feel lost and forgotten,

God of those who are orphaned and without a family,

God of the courageous who advocate for their families,

Remember your daughters today.

Remember those who do not feel like they fit in.

Remember the women who have a fierce love for their whole family.

Remember those made to feel small because of their gender.

Remember all who yearn to understand what it means for Jesus to be "God with us."

Closing prayers in this study are based on Rachel Asproth's "A Prayer for Women: Remember Your Daughters." Used by permission.

Student of Scripture

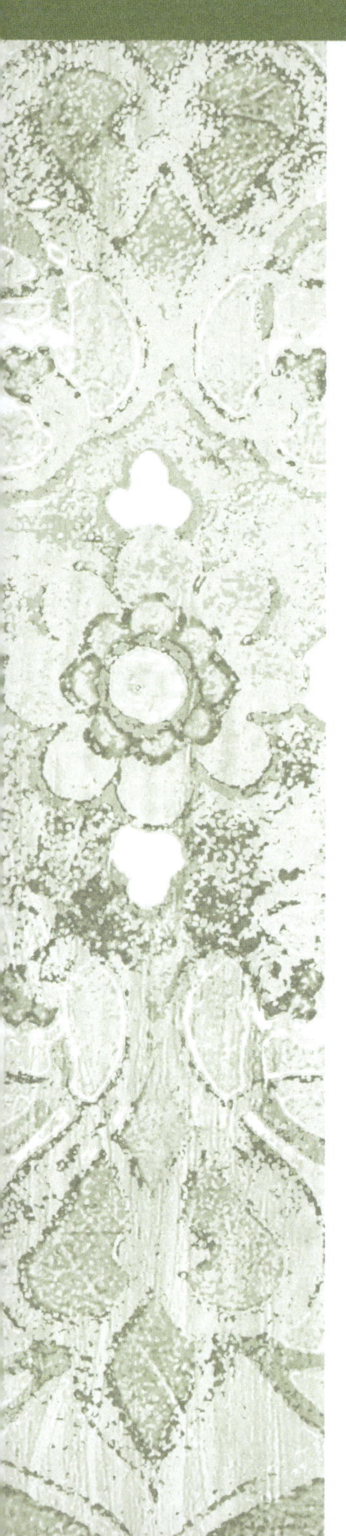

Mary of Nazareth

Mary, the mother of Jesus, is also known as Mary of Nazareth. What do you picture when you think of Mary? Perhaps you imagine a beautiful icon in an elaborate church, or maybe an actress playing a very pregnant Mary in your church's Nativity play. But have you ever thought of Mary as a poet and a student of theology?

In this session we are introduced to Mary as a young woman—before she gives birth to Jesus, raises him in Nazareth, and follows his ministry. She may have been between fourteen and sixteen years old, which to our modern mindset makes us think of her as a child. Yet her community would have considered her an adult. A young one, yes. But in Mary's society, women her age were ready to manage the logistics of a household.

The poetic song we are about to study provides insight into Mary's maturity despite her age. When faced with what would have seemed an improbable announcement of the role she would play in God's plan, Mary responded with a long confession of God's power and character. As you read her story, think about how she would have learned about these things.

Read It

Key Bible Passage

For this session, read Luke 1:26–56.

Optional Reading

Hannah's Story: 1 Samuel 1:1–2:11

The optional reading features the story of Hannah, an Israelite woman who lived long before Mary. She was barren, but after fervently praying to the Lord for a child, she gave birth to Samuel. After Hannah had weaned him, she took him to the tabernacle and sang a song (1 Sam. 2:1–10) as she dedicated him to the Lord's service. It's likely that Mary would have learned Hannah's song as she was growing up. Samuel served in the tabernacle and later became a great prophet in Israel.

"The Mighty One has done great things for me—holy is his name."

LUKE 1:49

Know It

1. Mary heard from an angel that she would give birth to "the Son of the Most High." Before she could feel in her womb the truth of the angel's words, she burst forth with the artistic poetry recorded in Luke 1:46–55. What strikes you as inspiring, confusing, or interesting about the words in Mary's song?

2. Mary names several characteristics of God in her song. Which of them, if any, surprise you? Why?

3. What do you imagine Mary felt as she said (or sang) these words?

Geography

Mary lived in Nazareth, a village built on a ridge line defined by two great valleys to its north and south. Archaeologists found the oldest ruins of Nazareth in a shallow basin where the soil is slightly chalky and without an abundance of water. These clues tell us that since the land could not support many people, Nazareth was considered a village and not a city.

Due to its location on the ridge, Nazareth was off the beaten path. From the edge of the ridge, one could look down onto the international roads that crisscrossed through the valleys. On any given day, Mary may have noticed Roman soldiers or caravans of traders on the roads.

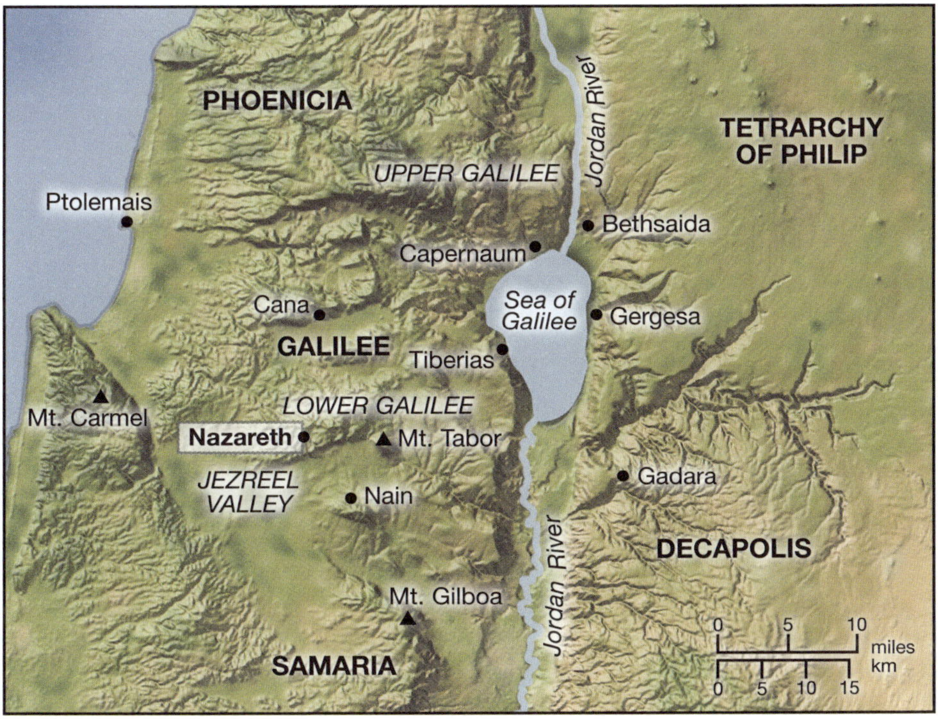

Mary's hometown was Nazareth, nestled on a ridge southwest of the Sea of Galilee

Since Nazareth wasn't situated on the main trade networks, no one "accidentally" passed through. People had to consciously make a choice to walk uphill to arrive at the village. Nazareth was a protected place where residents were able to preserve a traditional lifestyle without the outside pressures of larger society.

Archaeological remains at the Church of the Annunciation in Nazareth

When we think of places where God might find people who will make a dramatic impact on the world, we don't often think of small, out-of-the-way villages. Nazareth was not a player in the international scene. Mary's village was an unlikely place to find movers and shakers, and yet God saw a young woman there who had tremendous faith and an awful lot of courage!

History

Mary belonged to a long line of Israelites who had studied the words of the prophets, announcing that God would one day send his Messiah—someone God would use to restore his people and bring freedom from oppression. When Babylon, a foreign enemy, destroyed their land and took them into exile, a remnant of Jewish people returned to rebuild Jerusalem and their temple. They wondered, *Is this the time for God's promised restoration?* And yet in due time, more foreign rulers oppressed the Jewish nation. Eventually a new question arose: *Is this the extent of God's restoration?*

At every step when they thought they had regained what was lost in exile—land, independence, their temple, a king—the Jewish people saw glimmers of hope, but they questioned whether they were experiencing the fullness of what God had promised. When the angel Gabriel appeared to Mary, his message was not only that she would bear a son, but also that her son was God's answer to the Jewish longing for complete restoration.

Mary also belonged to a long tradition of men and women who sang hymns in response to God's involvement in their lives: Miriam, after God had destroyed Pharaoh's army (Exodus 15:19–21); Deborah, after God liberated the Israelites from Canaanite oppression (Judges 5:1–31); and Hannah, after God provided her with a son (1 Samuel 2:1–10). When Mary heard that God had chosen her to be the mother of the Jewish Messiah, she, too, burst into song. It's not surprising that she modeled her song after Hannah's. After all, their stories were similar—two women with unlikely pregnancies who were responding to God's work in their individual lives.

If Mary used Hannah's song as a model for her own, then think for a moment about its implications for Mary's understanding of Scripture. Someone must have taught her this rich understanding of how God works in the lives of individuals and the life of the community. Perhaps Mary's mom memorized and sang the songs of their ancestors. We may never know how repeating the songs of Miriam, Deborah, and Hannah influenced the formation of Mary's understanding of God, but the idea is certainly thought-provoking.

View from the top of Nazareth's ridgeline

SINGER	SCRIPTURE REF.	CIRCUMSTANCES	HIGHLIGHTS
Miriam	Exodus 15:19–21	The Israelites escaped the Egyptian army when the Lord parted the Red Sea. The Lord collapsed the water back onto the Egyptians.	Praises the Lord for saving Israel from their enemies.
Deborah and Barak	Judges 5:1–31	The Lord helped Israel defeat Sisera's army.	Praises the Lord for victory. Commends the Israelites who took a stand.
Hannah	1 Samuel 2:1–10	God answered Hannah's prayer for a son. Hannah kept her promise to dedicate Samuel to the Lord.	Praises God's holiness. Recognizes that God exalts the lowly and humbles the proud.
Mary	Luke 1:46–55	The angel Gabriel told Mary that through the Holy Spirit, she would give birth to Jesus.	Praises God for honoring her. Praises God for being merciful to Israel. Praises God for favoring the humble and punishing the proud.

Narrative

Gabriel Visits Mary

Our narrative begins with God sending the angel Gabriel to greet Mary and declare a promise: She would be the mother of the Messiah. The angel then reveals the role her son will fulfill. Notice how Gabriel describes that God is with her, and she has found great favor in God's sight (vv. 28–30). What a beautiful way to be addressed!

Mary was old enough to start a family but too young to be a respected elder in the community. She lived in a village that held traditional values. People in Nazareth were not influencers in politics, religion, or culture, yet the angel told Mary she was favored. She had been noticed by God, and he was already present with her. We can imagine how blessed Mary must have felt when she heard Gabriel's reassurance that she was seen and known by God.

The Annunciation, by Henry Ossawa Tanner

Gabriel then describes the roles her son will fill (vv. 31–33): His name will be Jesus. He will be great and called "the Son of the Most High." God will give him the throne of King David. He will reign forever over the house of Jacob, and his kingdom will have no end. Those are big roles for her son to fulfill!

Gabriel then mentions that Mary is not the only woman who is having an unlikely pregnancy: Her older cousin Elizabeth is also pregnant! Perhaps Gabriel wanted to show Mary how God was already in the process of making the miraculous happen.

The practical life experience of both the older woman and the younger suggests pregnancy was impossible—Elizabeth was past her childbearing years, and Mary was not yet married. Mary and Elizabeth were witnesses to each other, confirming that God was indeed doing something dramatic in both their lives.

Mary's Song

The fact that Mary understood the magnitude of Gabriel's message is reflected in the song she sings in verses 46–55. Mary reaches back through thousands of years of history to claim that God is still working to fulfill his promises. We could spend hours tracing the connections of Mary's song to the Old Testament, but for now, think about how this song reflects Mary's understanding of the Bible and God's character. Notice, too, that she must still wait through her pregnancy and Jesus' growing-up years to see what God's restoration will be like in real life. In this song, however, we see her declaration that God will be faithful to do what he promised.

Aerial view of the Church of the Annunciation, located in Nazareth's shallow basin

Bible References in Mary's Song (Luke 1:46–55)

MARY'S SONG	OLD TESTAMENT REFERENCES
"My soul glorifies the LORD and my spirit rejoices in God my Savior." (vv. 46–47)	"My heart rejoices in the Lord." (1 Sam. 2:1)
"He has been mindful of the humble state of his servant." (v. 48)	"He will guard the feet of his faithful servants." (1 Sam. 2:9)
"Holy is his name." (v. 49)	"Holy and awesome is his name." (Ps. 111:9)
"His mercy extends to those who fear him." (v. 50)	"The LORD's love is with those who fear him." (Ps. 103:17)
"He has performed mighty deeds with his arm." (v. 51)	"The arm of the LORD is not too short to save." (Isa. 59:1)
"He has scattered those who are proud ... [and] brought down rulers ... but has lifted up the humble." (vv. 51–52)	"Human pride [will be] brought low." (Isa. 2:11) "The arrogant [will be] humbled." (Isa. 5:15) "I the LORD bring down the tall tree and make the low tree grow tall." (Ezek. 17:24) "The lowly will be exalted and the exalted will be brought low." (Ezek. 21:26)
"He has filled the hungry with good things." (v. 53)	"He defends the cause of the fatherless and the widow." (Deut. 10:18) "I rescued the poor who cried for help." (Job 29:12) "Those who seek the LORD lack no good thing." (Ps. 34:10) "He ... fills the hungry with good things." (Ps. 107:9) "He ... gives food to the hungry." (Ps. 146:7)

Live It

In Mary's song, we see that she was more than the bearer of a miraculous child; she was a student of Scripture and a proclaimer of God's work. Remember, Mary would have taken the theology that we studied in her song and imparted it to Jesus. This is the mother who raised her son to change the world—indeed, a young woman to greatly admire. Whether you're a parent of biological or adopted children or a mentor to the younger generation, you have the potential to share significant theological lessons about who God is and what he promises. Like Mary, your life and your words will have a lasting impact on the people around you.

Life Application Questions

1. Both Mary's and Elizabeth's unique pregnancies led them to praise God, despite the likelihood their circumstances created some social awkwardness. Imagine and describe some ways they might have handled this pressure. Has God ever asked you to do something you were afraid others might question or criticize?

2. Have you ever felt that God gave you a unique gift or talent he wants you to use to benefit the people around you? Was your initial response similar or different to Mary's reaction?

3. Go back to the list of God's characteristics that you wrote down under question 2 in the "Know It" section. When you think of Jesus as the Messiah, do you think of these characteristics? Why or why not?

4. Who in your life is a witness to what God is doing through you? Like Elizabeth and Mary, do you encourage each other to wait with expectation to receive what God has promised, even when it seems impossible?

5. Have you been waiting for God to do something for you—maybe for many years? What do you imagine Mary would say to you about waiting?

Prayer

God of those in urban, suburban, and rural places,

God of those who wait with expectation and hope for you to come,

God of the humble and the hungry and the ignored,

God of the creative artists and those who are singers of songs,

Remember your daughters today.

Remember those who struggle to believe that you see them and are with them.

Remember the women who sing songs of hope, courage, and faith.

Remember those who need reminders of your fierce love and persistent presence.

Remember the women who accept your invitation to belong to your story despite how impossible it may seem.

Notes

A Faithful Witness

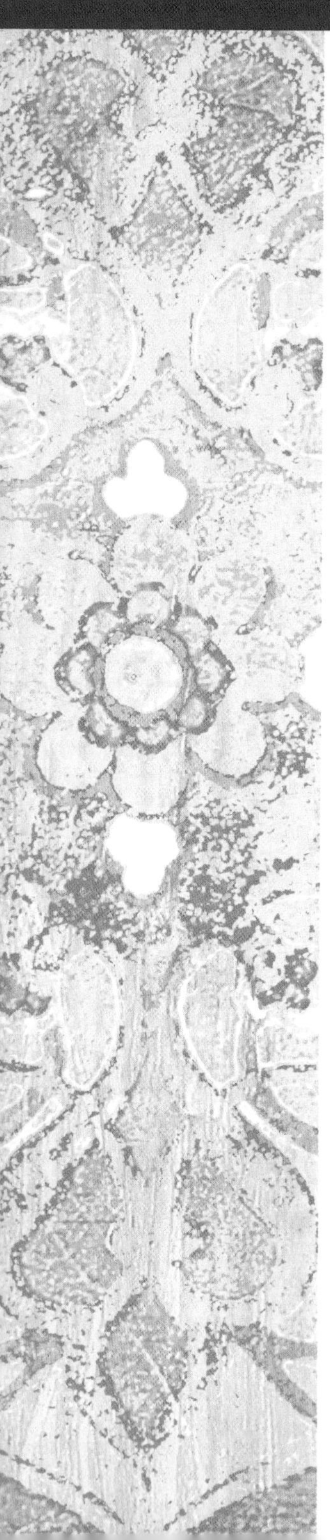

Anna

If you enjoy sharing God's Word with others, it's possible you've discovered that due to various factors, certain places or people have simply been off-limits or out of reach for your ministry. And depending on your age, some people may even refuse to listen to you simply because in their eyes, you're either too young or too old to speak with authority. Yet Anna's story, found in Luke's gospel right after the account of Jesus' birth, shows us that God often pushes on cultural boundaries and assumptions that have been established. The beginning of Luke 2 may sound familiar since it's often read every year at Christmastime. What happens further along, when Mary and Joseph take Jesus to the temple and encounter Simeon, may also be familiar to you. But Anna's story, which follows Simeon's, doesn't get quite as much attention. Anna is named in the text, but the words she speaks are not recorded. Let's discover Anna's encounter with the baby Jesus and think about her life.

Read It

Key Bible Passage

For this session, read Luke 2:21–38.

Optional Reading

A prophecy about the Messiah's ministry: Isaiah 42:1–9

A prophecy about his followers' ministry: Joel 2:28–29

The optional reading in Isaiah is a prophecy about God placing his Spirit upon the promised Messiah, Jesus, allowing him to "bring justice to the nations" (v. 1), healing to the sick, and freedom to the captives. The reading in Joel speaks of God pouring out his Spirit on all his children—young and old, men and women—empowering them to tell others about the wonderful work of Jesus. Anna is a beautiful example of this word being fulfilled.

"She gave thanks to God and spoke about the child to all who were looking forward to the redemption of Jerusalem."

LUKE 2:38

If you consider factors such as Simeon's and Anna's ages, spoken words, actions, and audience, how would you compare and contrast their roles in this passage?

	SIMEON (LUKE 2:25–35)	ANNA (LUKE 2:36–38)
How are they described?		
Why were they at the temple?		
What did they do upon seeing Jesus?		
What did they say—and to whom?		
How did they interact with Jesus' parents, Joseph and Mary?		

Explore It

Culture

Our study begins with a few important actions taken by Mary and Joseph after the birth of Jesus. Following the command in Leviticus 12:1–3, Mary and Joseph arrange for their son to be circumcised on the eighth day after his birth, at which time the child is named. This timing was practical, allowing eight days for the mother to recover and enough time to make sure the child would survive. Mary and Joseph follow God's instructions and name the infant Jesus.

Forty days after the birth of a male child, a Jewish mother was expected to go to the temple to dedicate her son to the Lord and offer sacrifices. Although the sacrifices were offered by the mother, Joseph accompanied Mary to the temple (Luke 2:22). Mary gave two birds (v. 24), which is an indication that Mary and Joseph did not have much money but still followed God's instructions.

Presentation at the Temple. Stained glass window in St. Michael Cathedral, Toronto

Geography

Luke 2 begins in Bethlehem, the same town where Naomi returned from Moab with Ruth, as we read about in session 1. During Mary's time, Bethlehem was a small town with a modest population. It functioned as a shepherding and farming community, where people ate the food they grew each year and did not store excess goods. Other than its fame as the birthplace of King David, Bethlehem didn't play a large role in Jewish life. The town sat in the shadow of the much larger city of Jerusalem, only five miles to the north.

In contrast to Bethlehem, Jerusalem was a large, urban area with a towering outside wall and ornately decorated buildings. Herod the Great built a large palace on the western side of the city, opposite the massive platform that supported the Jewish temple on the eastern side. Like most large cities, the wealthy lived in palatial houses and common people lived in small homes that were densely packed along narrow roads. Diverse people flocked there, and it was not unusual to see Roman soldiers walking the streets

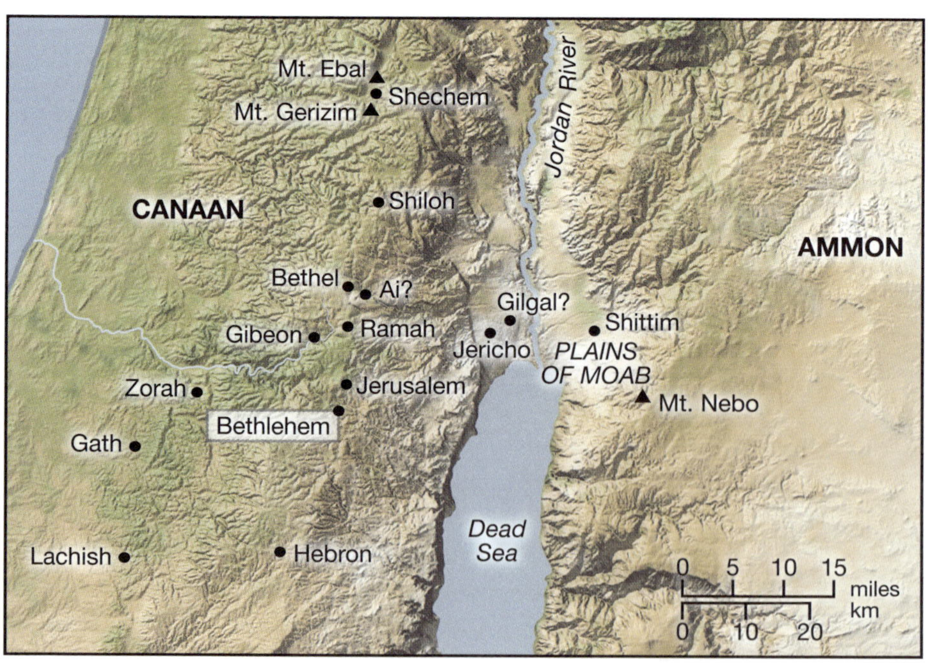

alongside Jewish priests. Large numbers of pilgrims swarmed the city during festivals, because no matter how far away a Jewish person lived from Jerusalem, it was still the one city in the world chosen by God to house his remarkable temple.

Both Bethlehem and Jerusalem preserved memories of King David—the former was his birthplace, and from the latter he ruled over all the Israelite tribes. Luke uses both locations to stoke the reader's curiosity about how this small human in the line of David will ultimately fulfill God's promises to restore his people. As we focus our attention on Jerusalem, we also meet two people who have waited their entire lives for that fulfillment.

Narrative

Mary and Joseph Meet Simeon

Mary and Joseph have gone to the temple to dedicate their firstborn son and present their purification offerings at the temple in Jerusalem. Here we meet Simeon, who had been waiting for the "consolation" (or restoration) of Israel. Luke tells us that "the Holy Spirit was on him," indicating he was a prophet (vv. 25–26). Simeon had likely waited his whole life to see how God would fulfill his promises in the Scriptures. Such incredible tenacity! Imagine faithfully waiting for decades, stubbornly believing God would finally act to right what was wrong. The Spirit had prompted him to go to the temple that day, and when he saw Mary, Joseph, and the infant Jesus, Simeon immediately recognized that a promise had been fulfilled in the child. In verse 32, he bursts out with a quote from the prophet Isaiah's message that God's salvation (Jesus) would be the glory of Israel and also reach gentiles—people who were not Jewish (Isa. 42:6; 49:6).

Anna Recognizes the Messiah

We meet Anna next. She does not have a direct speaking role, so it's easy for readers to ignore her. But she is meant to be noticed! Luke dedicates a lot of words to describing Anna. She is a prophetess, and while female prophets are not as commonly mentioned as male prophets, the Israelites remembered Miriam (Ex. 15:20–21), Deborah (Judg. 4–5), and Huldah (2 Kings 22:14–20) as influential prophetesses. In the book of Acts, Luke tells us that an evangelist named Philip had four daughters who were prophetesses (21:8–9). Anna fits into this line of unusual but not unheard-of female prophets.

Bethlehem

Luke also notes Anna's lineage. She is the daughter of Penuel of the tribe of Asher (2:36). This detail is significant! Asher's tribal land was located along the Mediterranean coast north of Mount Carmel. Long after King David's reign and Israel's division into a northern kingdom (called Israel) and a southern kingdom (called Judah), Asher's territory was among the first to be conquered by the fearsome Assyrian Empire. The northern Israelite tribes, which included the people of Asher, were exiled from their land. But some of those tribes went south and found refuge with Judah. Years later, the nation of Babylon conquered Judah, and the people there, too, were exiled. God promised he would restore Judah and Israel together (Ezek. 37:22–24; Amos 9:11; Acts 15:16)—so when Luke mentions that Anna was from Asher, he is indicating this child will bring salvation for *all* of God's people, not just the southern tribe of Judah.

There is yet another remarkable detail about Anna's life: She was married for a brief seven years, and then she was a widow "of" or "for" eighty-four years—the original Greek can be translated correctly using either of these two small prepositions. We can read that either Anna lived as a widow until she was eighty-four years old, or that she was widowed and then lived an additional eighty-four years. In either case, we can conclude with certainty that Anna was old. She dedicated her entire widowed life to fasting and praying in the temple. What joy she must have experienced when she saw the infant Jesus and realized he was the fulfillment of all of God's promises! One final detail about Anna: Although her precise words are not recorded, Anna gave thanks to God and then turned to speak "to all who were looking forward to the redemption of Jerusalem" (2:38).

The Pairing of Simeon and Anna

Part of Luke's unique style is the way he creates pairs of characters who together reflect aspects of who Jesus is:

PAIRINGS IN LUKE 1–2	
Gabriel announces a miraculous birth to two relatives	**Zechariah / Elizabeth** (1:11–20; baby: John the Baptist) and **Mary** (1:26–38; baby: Jesus)
Song of salvation	**Zechariah** (1:67–79) and **Mary** (1:46–55)
Davidic cities	**Bethlehem** (2:4) and **Jerusalem** (2:22)
Encounters with prophets at the temple	**Simeon** (2:25–35) and **Anna** (2:36–38)

When we read about Simeon and Anna together, we observe an example of two people who had waited their entire lives to see God's promises fulfilled. Because they were actively watching, they noticed right away when God acted. In Simeon we see that God's restoration will reach all the gentiles, and in Anna we notice that God's restoration is for all the people of Israel. Simeon has a speaking role, but his message is given in private to Mary and Joseph. Anna also speaks, but publicly to all who will listen. It is only fitting that the inclusive gospel message is put into the mouths of a male and a female character.

Live It

Anna's persistence to believe that God would fulfill his promises can be a huge encouragement to those of us who long to see God work sooner rather than later. She had the voice of wisdom and was not afraid to proclaim God's goodness.

Life Application Questions

1. We don't know the exact words Anna said, but from reading the context, what would you guess she might have said "to all who were looking forward to the redemption of Jerusalem" (v. 38)?

2. Do you have people in your life who are like Simeon or Anna—mature believers who have deep roots of faith and are quick to recognize when God is present? If so, describe how they have influenced your life.

3. Like Anna, have you ever waited a long time to see God's promises fulfilled? What helps you wait with faithfulness and expectation?

4. Have circumstances or people in your life wrongly given you the message that God uses only certain people to witness to his work in the world? What can Anna teach us about who and what God values?

5. In what fresh ways can you imitate Anna's devotion to God, her attentiveness to the Scriptures, and their relevance to life today? Are there others in your life who would benefit from hearing about what God shows you?

Prayer

God of those who wait faithfully through troubling years,

God of infants, young parents, and widows,

God of those who are considered lost but who are waiting for your restoration,

God of women who are silenced due to gender, age, or status,

Remember your daughters today.

Remember those who faithfully wait their whole lives for you to fulfill your promises.

Remember the women who feel silenced and irrelevant.

Remember the women who boldly witness to your powerful deeds.

Remember all who ache to see restoration in their communities.

Notes

4 THE WOMAN AT THE WELL

Her Remarkable Encounter

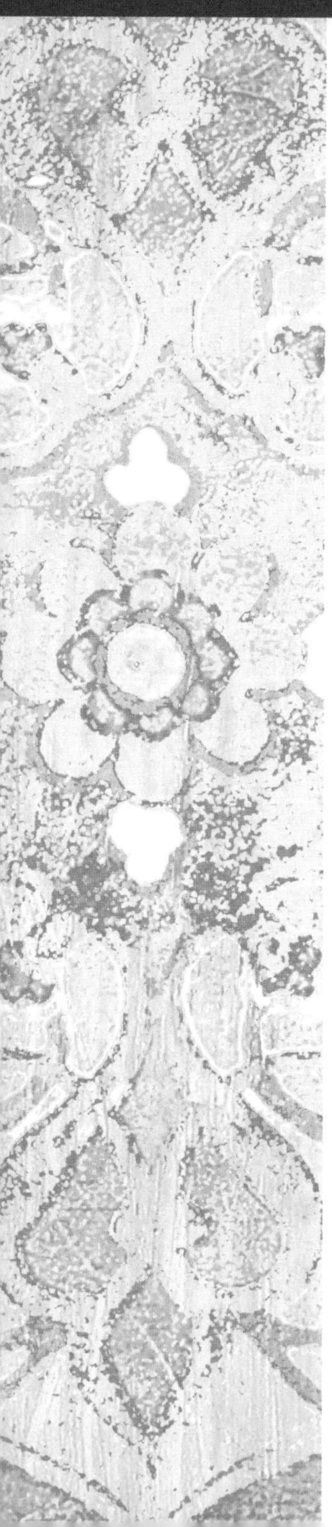

The Woman at the Well

When you hear the phrase "the woman at the well," do any images immediately come to mind based on past teachings you've heard about this Samaritan woman? Sometimes we latch onto one detail and ignore the rest of her story. But this unnamed woman has a remarkable role in the gospel of John. She initiates a complex theological conversation with Jesus, and she becomes the first evangelist to the Samaritans.

There is a lot of context in this passage that the original audience intuitively understood—information like the location of the ancient roads, the cultural differences between the Samaritans and the Jewish people, and even how people collected water. Everything is important, and the more you dig into the background, the more astounding the narrative becomes. When you read through this story, take note of small details and make a list of as many questions as you can about this fascinating woman.

Key Bible Passage

For this session, read John 4:1–30, 39–42.

Optional Reading

The origin of the Samaritan people: 2 Kings 17:24–41

The optional reading explains how the king of Assyria deported the people from the northern kingdom of Israel, then repopulated the land with foreigners who worshiped other gods. In Jesus' day, the former area of the northern kingdom was known as Samaria, and the Jewish people despised the idolatrous practices of its inhabitants. This history helps us understand the cultural nuances surrounding Jesus' interaction with the Samaritan woman at the well.

"Many of the Samaritans from that town believed in [Jesus] because of the woman's testimony."

JOHN 4:39

Know It

1. As you read this Bible passage, list some words that you think would describe the Samaritan woman, and identify what made you choose those words.

2. When you picture this scene, about how old do you imagine this woman was? Why?

3. Why do you think the Samaritan woman's testimony had such a strong impact on her community that they would drop their daily activities to talk to Jesus?

Geography and History

Geography and history play a significant role in the story of the Samaritan woman, and to fully understand both, we must go back to the Old Testament. Hold on tight for a mad dash through history!

The Divided Kingdom

For a short time, the Israelite tribes were united under one king—first David, then his son Solomon, then Solomon's son Rehoboam. During Rehoboam's reign, the northern tribes tired of his high taxes and harsh policies, so they rebelled and declared their independence. In the resulting split, the northern kingdom was called "Israel" and the southern kingdom "Judah."

The Assyrian Invasion

In 722 BC, the Assyrians demolished the city of Samaria, the capital of the northern kingdom, and took most of the Israelites into exile. The Assyrians also brought in people captured from other places, where false gods were worshiped. Several years later, some of them adopted beliefs that were similar to the Israelites' (2 Kings 17:24–41). These people, with mixed backgrounds and beliefs, became known as Samaritans.

Judah's Exile and Return

In 586 BC, the Babylonian Empire destroyed Jerusalem and exiled its residents to Babylon. When the Persian Empire conquered Babylon, the new ruler, Cyrus, allowed the Jewish people to return to Jerusalem based on the claim they were God's people. The Samaritans, however, made similar claims but added they were the faithful ones who had never left the land. Animosity developed between the two groups when the Jewish people starting rebuilding the temple in Jerusalem (Ezra 4–6; Neh. 2:10–20; 4:1–15) and reached its climax during the time of Jesus.

Two Temples

After the temple in Jerusalem was rebuilt, Greece became the dominant power. The Samaritans who had rejected the Jewish temple received permission to build their own temple on Mount Gerizim. Now each of these groups who claimed to be God's chosen people had their own temples! Roughly three hundred years after the Samaritans built their temple, the Jewish people fought a dramatic battle against Greece and earned their independence. They expanded their kingdom into Samaritan territory and destroyed the temple on Mount Gerizim. Just over one hundred years later, a Jewish man named Jesus sat at the foot of Mount Gerizim, in the heart of Samaritan territory, and had a theological conversation with a Samaritan woman about how and where to worship God. What a remarkable encounter given the history of conflict between the Jewish people and Samaritans!

Narrative

The Samaritan Road (vv. 1–4)

John 4:3–4 makes a simple statement that Jesus left Judea to go to Galilee, and that "he had to go through Samaria." When you understand the network of roads during that time, you'll see why this is a notable phrase. Samaria was sandwiched between the regions of Judea and Galilee, and a road connecting both went through its territory. But there was also a connecting road that *didn't* take travelers through Samaria; it ran from Jerusalem to Jericho and then north along the Jordan River. Since Jesus had a choice of which road to take, the fact that "he had to go through Samaria" makes readers think Jesus had *planned* for this meeting between him and the woman—or at least that God had directed him to take the Samaritan road.

SYRIA
PHOENICIA
Mt. Hermon
Mediterranean Sea
Tyre
Caesarea Philippi
TETRARCHY OF PHILIP
Mt. of Beatitudes
Ptolemais
Bethsaida
Capernaum
Cana
Sea of Galilee
Tiberias
Dion?
Mt. Carmel
GALILEE
Mt. Tabor
Nazareth
Gadara
Nain
Caesarea
Mt. Gilboa
Road through Samaria
Salim?
DECAPOLIS
SAMARIA
Samaria
Jordan River
Sychar
Gerasa
Mt. Gerizim
Jordan River Route
Antipatris
Joppa
Arimathea
PEREA
Ephraim
Lydda
JUDEA
Philadelphia
Jericho
Emmaus?
Bethany
Azotus
Bethphage?
("Beyond the Jordan")
Jerusalem
Bethany
Bethlehem
Qumran
Ashkelon
Machaerus
Dead Sea
Hebron
En Gedi
NABATEA
IDUMEA
Masada
Beersheba
0 10 20 miles
0 10 20 30 km

Challenging the Assumptions (vv. 5–9)

After walking for several hours, Jesus and his disciples stopped for a break in Samaritan territory. The disciples went to find food in the nearby village of Sychar, which left Jesus alone, waiting and resting at a well while a woman came to collect water. Historically, people have assumed she was ashamed of her life and went to the well at noon since, during the heat of the day, it was less likely she would encounter others. Another popular assumption is that she was by herself because other women in the village shunned her.

Entrance to the traditional site of Jacob's Well (photo c. 1890–1900)

Yet there is no evidence to support these claims. Women went to the well whenever they needed to. We don't know why she went this particular time, but we know she was performing a daily task when she encountered Jesus. Remarkably, Jesus asked to drink some of the water she pulled from the well. She was startled that a Jewish man would initiate a conversation with her, a Samaritan woman (v. 9). Still, she continued to engage in the conversation, only to be surprised once again when Jesus stated that *she* should be asking *him* for a drink. What a puzzling thing to say!

Living Water? (vv. 10–15)

Even more strange is Jesus' next statement that he could give her "living water." This is where it's helpful for us—a modern audience with easy access to filtered water—to realize the land of the Bible was mostly dry and without reliable access to clean water. People had to carefully manage the water they collected from three common sources: springs, wells, and cisterns.

Jesus and the Samaritan woman met at a community well, but notice what kind of water Jesus offered—living water! This kind of water came from a spring, but without one nearby, the woman was understandably confused. Jesus went on to say that those who drink his living water will never thirst again—another amazing claim! Within minutes of meeting, their roles had changed. The woman became the one seeking life-sustaining water, and Jesus offered himself as the source of all life.

The Context of Ancient Culture (vv. 16–17)

The next few verses are often misunderstood, because too often we don't read them according to ancient culture. When Jesus told the woman to get her husband, she honestly replied that she had no husband. Jesus pressed into what had to be a difficult subject for her. He revealed that she had been married five times and now lived with someone who wasn't her husband. In a modern context, this sounds like she was a flighty gold digger with a habit of divorcing—and now she was living with someone she hadn't married. But divorce was rare at the time, and people certainly didn't divorce casually.

Hellenistic-era house on Mt. Gerizim, possibly the home of a Samaritan priest

Yet the mention of five husbands is perplexing because it is so unusual. It's possible that one marriage ended in divorce, but it's culturally unlikely that five husbands divorced her! More likely is that more than one of her husbands died. The fact that she remarried several times is a cultural cue that she couldn't support herself and most likely did not have children who could support her. Remember, this was a patriarchal society, where inheritances passed to male members of the family. So with a history of five husbands, she might have remarried out of necessity. Her suffering was not private either. In this small village, people would have known what was going on in her life. And while we don't know how old she was, with this many marriages, chances are high that she was one of the older women in the village.

Another challenging question arises when we read that the man she was living with was not her husband. It's possible she lived with a male relative, but whatever the case, we can safely assume she lived a hard, sorrowful life. When Jesus said to her, "You have had five husbands, and the man you now have is not your husband," notice how the Samaritan woman acknowledged the truth but did not become defensive. Jesus had identified an area of true distress in her life without making her feel ashamed.

A Theological Debate (vv. 19–26)

Next, the Samaritan woman engaged Jesus in a theological debate: At whose temple was the right place to worship? Jesus stated that salvation came from the Jewish people and announced that God was transforming true worship into something new and inclusive. In reply, the woman said the Messiah would reveal the truth of what God was doing. What's interesting here is that Samaritans did not have an established hope in a coming Messiah like the Jewish people did. The woman was making a distinct effort to answer Jesus according to his Jewish tradition, creating an opening for Jesus to reveal that *he* was the expected Messiah.

Sharing the Good News (vv. 27–30, 39–42)

When the Samaritan woman heard this news, she ran to share the amazing revelation with her community. She must have delivered her report in an encouraging manner, because many of the villagers made their way to the well to talk with this Jewish man. When the disciples returned from buying food, it seems that no one from the village wanted to tag along. Yet when *the woman* returned, she brought lots of people with her! And because she willingly shared about her encounter, the villagers asked Jesus and his disciples to stay for two days so they could enjoy fellowship.

The Samaritan woman is indeed remarkable. She overcame cultural barriers to embrace a unique opportunity to meet with Jesus. She understood Scripture but still had questions of theological significance. When she probed the meaning of Jesus' words and realized the implications of who he was, she ran to tell her community, leading many to discover that this Jewish man was indeed "the Savior of the world."

Mt. Gerizim *(l)* and Mt. Ebal *(r)*, near the ancient village of Sychar and present-day Nablus

Three Types of Water

1. Spring Water
Spring water was the absolute best because it was cool, filtered, and refreshing. The Israelites referred to fresh, flowing water as "living water," and since it was such a valuable commodity, they also referred to God as "the spring of living water" (Jer. 2:13).

2. Well Water
The next best water came from a well, but it required more effort to collect because each gallon weighed over eight pounds. Just think of the workout required for everyone in the family to drink!

3. Cistern Water
During the rainy season, families collected runoff water in a cistern—a hole dug in the ground and finished with plastered walls. They had to carefully use that precious volume of stagnant water throughout the dry season.

Ruins of a cistern from Qumran, an ancient settlement by the Dead Sea c. 100 BC

Live It

Like the Samaritan woman, we are often consumed with the challenging tasks of life. When Jesus asks for some of your time and effort, do you stop to ask more questions and probe the meaning of his request? Is it comforting to know he sees the painful parts of your life, or do you want to hide instead? This astonishing woman brought her full self into the conversation with Jesus, interacting with his words and becoming the bridge that connected Jesus with her larger community.

Life Application Questions

1. How has your view of the Samaritan woman at the well changed after this study?

2. Try to modernize this story by identifying two people groups who differ culturally, ethnically, or religiously and have a long history of animosity between them. In what ways does the story of the Samaritan woman at the well show us how their particular rifts might be healed?

3. Sometimes we think encounters with God will occur in special moments in special places; yet the Samaritan woman was in the middle of her day's work. When has God interrupted the normality of your day to call attention to something he wanted to show you? How did you respond?

4. Have you ever felt that circumstances distanced you from God or prevented you from doing great things for him? If so, try to imagine meeting Jesus at the well, just as the Samaritan woman did. What would he say to you, and how would you react?

5. Has Jesus revealed anything to you lately that would be worth sharing with your "village"—those in your sphere of influence—as a word of encouragement to them?

Prayer

God of the diversity of people worldwide,

God of women experiencing deep sorrow,

God of the married, divorced, single, and widowed,

God of those who seek your face,

Remember your daughters today.

Remember those who thirst deeply for your truth.

Remember the ones who have been silenced by their community but whom you see.

Remember the women who engage people despite cultural differences.

Remember those who share the good news about you with others.

5 MARY AND MARTHA

Sisters of Devotion and Hospitality

Mary and Martha

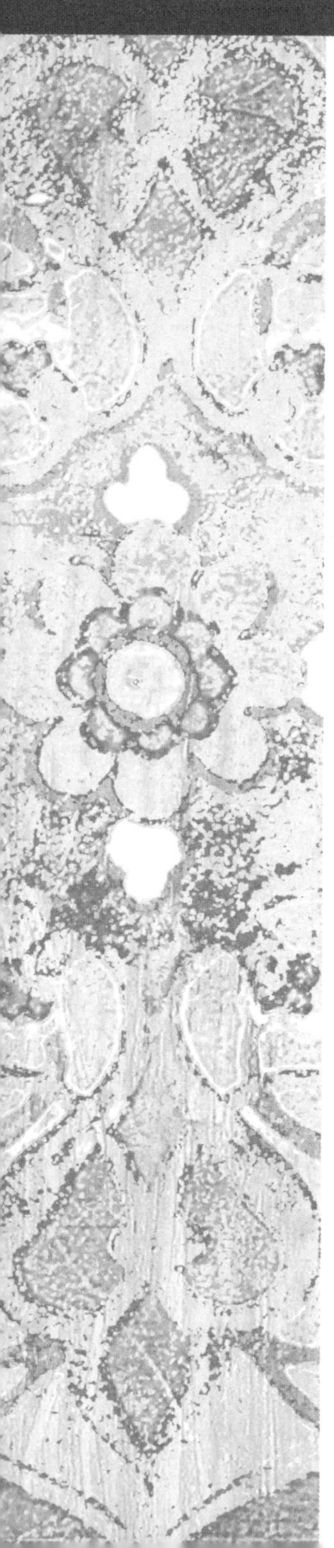

We are about to meet two sisters, Mary and Martha. They have a brother, Lazarus, but he is absent from the story in Luke 10. If you've read this passage before, what do you think of these two sisters? Are there character traits you associate with either of them? Sometimes when this story is retold, people focus on pitting Mary and Martha against each other to distinguish the responsible one from the troublemaker. But we are going to use a different approach.

Luke is the only gospel writer to include this particular story. He mentions both women by name, but he only records the words shared between Martha and Jesus. As we learned in session 3, Luke pairs people together for a specific purpose. In this study, we'll resist the urge to put these sisters in competition with each other or to reduce this story to a lesson that is only for women. Instead, we'll look for what this story reveals about how *anyone* should respond to Jesus and his teachings—a lesson that just happens to come through these women. Let's lean in.

Read It

Key Bible Passage

For this session, read Luke 10:38–42.

Optional Reading

The death and resurrection of Lazarus: John 11:1–46.

The optional reading offers another story involving Martha and Mary. It highlights the love they had for their brother, Lazarus; their sadness when he died; and their faith in Jesus' power over death. It also shows us the depth of love Jesus had for this family of three—and his own grief as he mourned alongside Mary and Martha.

"Jesus ... came to a village where a woman named Martha opened her home to him. She had a sister called Mary."

LUKE 10:38–39

1. Who in this story do you find yourself gravitating toward and relating to the most?

2. If you were an actor speaking Jesus' words out loud, what intonation would you use? How does this text resonate with you if you say his words with compassion? Try again with rebuke in your voice, then with a tone of understanding. As you repeat Jesus' words, what phrases stick out to you?

TONE	THOUGHTS THAT OCCUR TO YOU	PHRASES THAT STICK OUT
Compassion		
Rebuke		
Understanding		

3. What is the "one thing" Jesus says is needed (v. 42)?

Explore It

Geography

Although not specified in this story, Martha and Mary lived in Bethany, a small town perched near the top of the Mount of Olives, roughly two miles from Jerusalem. Although it was a short distance to Jerusalem, the road in between included the steep slope of the western side of the Mount of Olives. We meet Martha when she invites Jesus, and all the disciples following him, into her home. It's unclear whether this is the first time Martha has opened her home to them, but it is certainly not the last. Jesus and his disciples often traveled to Jerusalem to celebrate the Jewish festivals, and like other pilgrims, they had to find rooms to stay in. Jesus was in Martha's home often enough to develop a deep relationship with the family. He even considered their brother, Lazarus, a dearly loved friend (John 11:3, 11). We also see that in the final week of his life, Jesus and the disciples walk into Jerusalem in the morning and then leave for what we assume to be Martha's house in the evening. It is not far-fetched to guess that Martha offered hospitality to Jesus every time he came to Jerusalem.

Western slope of the Mt. of Olives

Culture

We sometimes think of first-century Jewish society as rigidly divided according to gender. Certainly there was an unequal distribution of authority, but men and women still shared several common spaces. Of course, there were jobs that only women fulfilled, like midwife or wet nurse. But other jobs were shared by men and women, from working in the fields to buying and selling goods at the market. Cooking and entertaining guests were also tasks shared by both men and women since acts of hospitality were highly valued. Rabbis used the story of Abraham rushing to offer hospitality to three guests (Gen. 18) to teach the importance of offering strangers food and drink and a place to stay. Hosts were honored to open their houses, and guests were expected to express gratitude and avoid creating additional work for their hosts.

One unique cultural detail in this story is that Martha is the one to invite Jesus into *her* home. We noticed in previous sessions that society was generally organized around the patriarch of the family, and we don't have enough details to conclude why Martha is recognized as the leader of the house. Perhaps she was single or her father had died. Her brother, Lazarus, is not mentioned in this story, which might suggest he hasn't taken over as head of the household. Maybe he is significantly younger than his sisters.

Christ in the House of Martha and Mary, by Henryk Siemiradzki

It would be nice to have these details, but neither Luke nor John solve the mystery for us in their gospels. Yet we do know they place the sisters in their narratives so we can learn from them.

Narrative

Our passage opens with Jesus and his disciples traveling up the Mount of Olives into the town of Bethany. Martha was quick to offer her home and hospitality to the teacher and his disciples, along with anyone in her community who wanted to learn from Jesus (Luke 10:38). Mary joined the group (v. 39), and although her words are not recorded, she likely would have engaged Jesus in conversation since it was common for people to ask questions and probe the meaning of the teacher's words.

It's hard to say how much time passes in this narrative—it could have been ten minutes, five hours, or two days. When Martha was distracted by all her preparations, we don't know whether she voiced her concern to everyone in the room or pulled Jesus aside and asked him to encourage Mary to help her. Luke passes over all these details to get to the dialogue.

First, Martha approached Jesus and addressed him as "Lord"—a title of respect for her guest of honor. She continued with a question: "Don't you care that my sister has left me to do the work by myself?" (v. 40). For anyone who has ever held all the responsibility for hosting a crowd, it's easy to imagine the fatigue and frustration reflected in Martha's question.

Martha then pressed Jesus to do something for her. "Tell her to help me!" she implored. The statement comes across as, "If you care, then you'll do something." Jesus responded as he often did when urged to behave a certain way—by refocusing attention on the real problem and need (vv. 41–42).

Something interesting was going on: Jesus had received Martha's hospitality, but when it was compared to the importance of engaging with his teachings, he pointed out the more valuable option. Jesus did not refuse Martha's hospitality nor say that what she was doing was inappropriate. Instead, he refocused her on his teachings since they would remain long after the results of her preparations. Interestingly, the story ends abruptly, and we're left wondering what Martha did in response to Jesus' words.

Martha took on the respected role of offering generous hospitality to a traveling rabbi, and Mary also had a respected role as a disciple sitting at Jesus' feet. Both are valuable, but Martha seems to be distracted by her tasks instead of properly prioritizing Jesus over everything else.

Bible Study in Bible Times

Education in the Scriptures was a high priority in ancient Jewish culture. Children learned Scripture from their parents and memorized it at the local synagogue. Learning was valued as a lifelong pursuit, so the community came together on the Sabbath to study the Bible. People did not sit silently and absorb a lecture or sermon; instead, skilled teachers engaged them with questions so they could learn through active participation. It was also not uncommon to gather in homes for study during the week. One rabbinic writing, dating not long after the time of Jesus, reflects the priority that learning held in the Jewish community: "Let your house be a meeting place for the sages, and sit in the very dust at their feet and thirstily drink in their words" (Avot 1:4). Luke records at least two other instances where men and women were listening to Jesus and participating in the conversation (8:19–21; 11:27–28). The setting in Luke 10, with Mary sitting "at the Lord's feet" and learning from him, would have been a common and valued place for both men and women.

Jewish women of Jesus' time did not have all the same freedoms as men, but they were present and active in their communities, studying Scripture together and offering hospitality. The key passage begins with two sisters who were both playing important roles: hosting a visiting teacher and sitting at his feet to learn from him. Mary and Martha call our attention to an age-old problem: how to balance obligations to others with cultivating and maintaining a close relationship with God. Working hard to offer hospitality and lead and care for others is a highly valued characteristic, but this story asks whether we are focused more on duties than we are on Jesus. Maybe along with Martha we can hear the understanding voice of Jesus say to us, "You are distracted by so many things. Focus instead on me."

Life Application Questions

1. In verse 42, Jesus tells Martha "there is only one thing worth being concerned about" and that "it will not be taken away" (NLT). How would you explain the "one thing"? How is that one thing never taken away?

2. If you could step into the story right where it ends, how would you interact with Martha? What questions would you have for Jesus?

3. How does Martha's boldness with Jesus and his kind response strike you? What new insights occur to you about Jesus' character? Do they prompt you to be more free in how you approach him?

4. What are some of the obligations in your own life that scream for your attention and devotion? How do you balance those expectations with focusing on Jesus?

5. Think of one of your own sisters. Maybe she is a biological sister, a "sister in Christ," or a dear friend who is as close as a sister. How do you see God working in her life? Have you shared those observations with her?

Prayer

God of the women who are exhausted by the expectations of others,

God of the women who generously open their homes and offer hospitality to others,

God of the women who hunger and thirst for your presence,

God of the silent, the outspoken, the questioners, and the ponderers,

Remember your daughters today.

Remember those who selflessly work to improve the lives of others.

Remember all your disciples who passionately study your Word.

Remember those who struggle to balance all of life's demands.

Remember the ones who need a private moment with you to hear you say they matter.

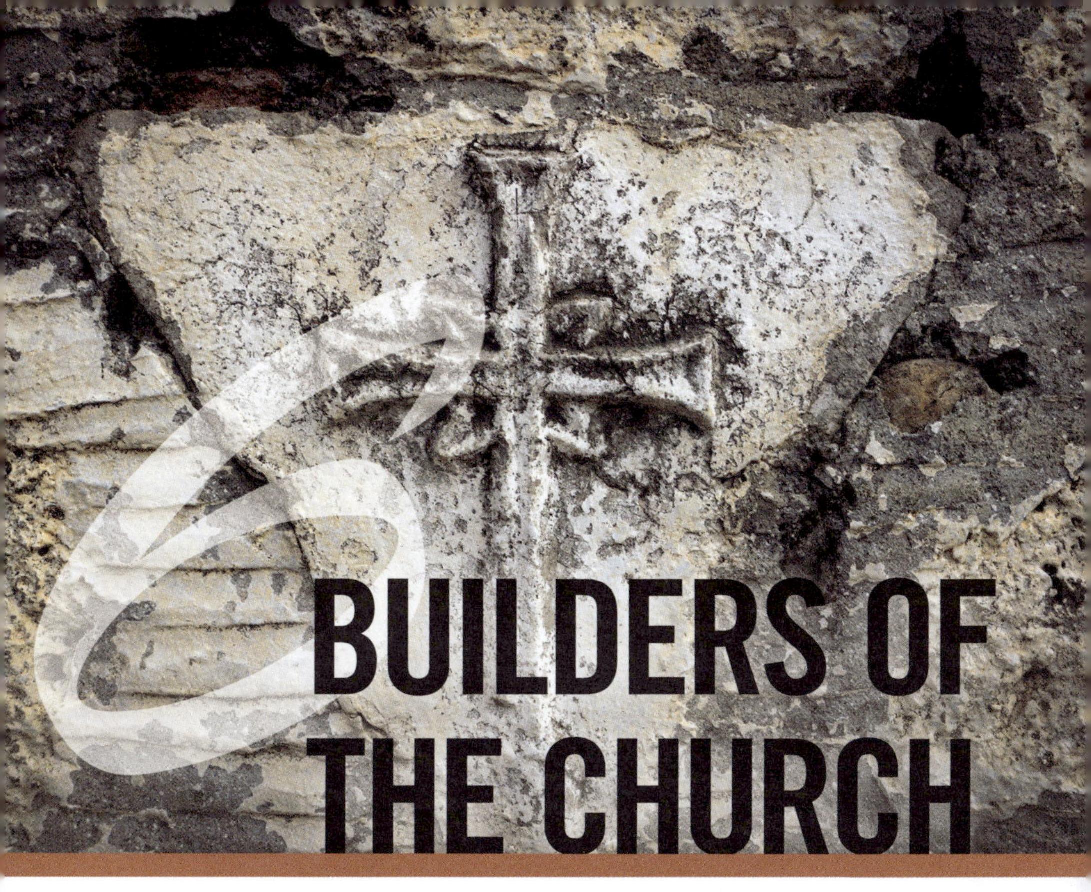

The Women of Romans 16

Builders of the Church

We began our study in Matthew's gospel, focusing on the mothers of Jesus, whose stories remind us that God works through all kinds of people to accomplish his purposes. Today we end with another list of names—colleagues and partners whom Paul acknowledged publicly for their help. Like the genealogy in Matthew, this list is easy to overlook. Resist the urge to do so, because it contains some interesting information about how women played important roles in the formation and growth of the early church. Each name represents the life of a unique person and their efforts over many years to support Paul's work to spread the gospel.

The book of Romans is best described as a letter composed by Paul with the intention it would be passed around to several Christian congregations in Rome. A notoriously dense text written in approximately 57 AD, Paul clarifies issues of theology with a focus on the complicated relationship between the early Jewish and gentile believers. At the end, Paul takes time to add a few personal touches by giving his own "shout-outs" to important people—and nearly a third of them are women! Let's dig in to find some hidden gems.

Read It

Key Bible Passage

For this session, read Romans 16:1–27.

Optional Reading

Insight into the ministry of Priscilla and Aquila: Acts 18:1–4, 18–26

The optional reading focuses on the background story of Priscilla and Aquila, a couple whom Paul greets in verse 3 of our key passage. They became Paul's ministry partners in Corinth, when they met him on his second missionary journey. Priscilla and Aquila went with Paul to Ephesus, where they discipled a Jewish man named Apollos. Apollos eventually moved to Corinth, where he encouraged the church there and used the Scriptures to prove to the Jewish people that Jesus was Israel's promised Messiah.

"I commend to you Phoebe our sister, who is [also] a minister of the church at Cenchreae."

ROMANS 16:1 NAB

Below is a list of the female names mentioned in this passage. Write next to each name any words Paul used to describe them. What do his descriptions tell you about the involvement and influence of women in the early church? Do any of these revelations surprise you or puzzle you? If so, why?

ROM. 16	NAME	DESCRIPTION	COMMENTS
vv. 1–2	Phoebe		
vv. 3–5	Priscilla		
v. 6	Mary		
v. 7	Junia		
v. 12	Tryphena and Tryphosa		
v. 12	Persis		
v. 13	Mother of Rufus		
v. 15	Julia		
v. 15	Sister of Nereus		

History and Culture

For the first time in this Bible study, we're stepping out of the traditional land of the Bible, where the Jewish worldview is known and accepted, and venturing to the heart of the Roman Empire, where it's dangerous to be a Jewish person or a Christian since their beliefs were thought to undermine the Roman government's authority.

The book of Acts gives us much of the backstory for Paul's letter to the Roman church. It tells us about Paul's efforts to take the gospel farther west into the Roman Empire. When Paul entered new cities to tell people about the Messiah, he preached first at the Jewish synagogues and then to the gentile residents. This was a remarkable endeavor because Paul had to teach gentiles about a Jewish Messiah, and they did not have the same comprehension of Jewish history or Scripture.

Roman empire at the time of Acts

Even more challenging was figuring out what to do when Paul's audience believed the message. The Jewish people and gentiles had completely different backgrounds and assumptions about how communities worked. Yet although they held different traditions and worldviews, Paul asked them to come together as one church.

Ruins of the first-century synagogue at Rome's ancient seaport

A significant barrier to creating unity was the importance of *status* in Roman society. Who you were in a particular family, along with your family's wealth, dictated whether you had access to education, whom you could marry, what job opportunities were available, and your political clout. Status was even more important than gender. A woman of high status had more opportunities than a male slave. Among people of equal status, men had more authority and were considered superior to women. Men exuded visible power and authority in public spheres, and women held leadership positions in the home.

Another significant cultural reality throughout the Roman Empire was the saturating presence of the gods they worshiped. Each city had a primary deity, although temples dedicated to several gods were prominent everywhere. The concepts of *god* and *city* were inseparable, so to offend one was to offend the other. Divine celebration days shaped how people observed the seasons. Stadiums, amphitheaters, and gymnasiums focused cultural attention on the gods. Their images were depicted in statues, and their names were written into official oaths and contracts. The gods were simply everywhere.

Think of the radical nature of the gospel in the Roman context. To reject the gods was to threaten the cultural identity of the people. Some believed the countercultural Jesus movement would upset the political and social arenas. Everyone, no matter their status, was invited to follow Jesus and take on his servant-leader characteristics.

As Christianity spread, believers began to gather in homes. They were a small minority in a culture that had shockingly different priorities. Coming together gave them an opportunity to be educated in shaping their lives around the Scriptures. Most likely those of independent means were the people who were able to offer hospitality. In a society that valued a person's status, the act of gathering together without consideration for whether someone was male, female, Jewish, or gentile was truly remarkable!

It was to these types of communities throughout Rome that Paul addressed his letter—with one more added challenge. Some years prior, Emperor Claudius had decided the Jewish people in Rome were troublemakers, so he expelled them from the city. The Jewish believers had to leave, while the gentile believers were allowed to stay and continue spreading the gospel. Several years later, when Claudius's edict was lifted and Jewish people returned to Rome, there was a rift between the gentile and Jewish believers in the church. Much of the dense theology in Paul's letter emerges from his explanation about why these two groups must exist together in harmony.

Sculpture of Roman gods and emperors

Narrative

A list of names at the end of a letter is not really a "narrative," but this one in particular can have a huge impact on the church today. You're already aware that almost a third of the names are female and that most of those names include a description of the role they played in the Roman church. Paul not only knew of but also *expected* women to be involved in the leadership of the growing church.

Little is known about Mary, Tryphena, and Tryphosa (vv. 6, 12) nor what they did to be considered women who were working "hard" for the Lord. Likewise, we do not know a lot about Rufus's mother except that she treated Paul like a son (v. 13). Three women in this list, however, stand out because Paul describes them as remarkable leaders: Phoebe, Priscilla, and Junia.

Phoebe (vv. 1–2)

In the original Greek, Paul describes Phoebe as *diakonos* (16:1). This word has a slightly different meaning based on its context. Within a household, *diakonos* can mean a "servant." In the public sphere or in a religious guild, *diakonos* can mean "attendant" or "official." If *diakonos* referred to a person who was serving a god, it meant "agent, authority, or courier." In other words, the status of the *diakonos* came from the person or organization they served. Interestingly, since Paul used this same word in 1 Corinthians 3:5 to describe the role he and Apollos had in the church, we can likely conclude that Phoebe was an official minister in the early church.

Paul mentions Phoebe first in his list, indicating she most likely carried Paul's letter to Rome. She would have been a woman of independent means who was able to pay for her travels. Some scholars suggest Phoebe may have also financially supported Paul. As the carrier of the letter, it's quite possible she would have read it out loud to the congregations in Rome. If any questions arose, Phoebe would have been the one to interpret Paul's theologically dense words.

Priscilla (vv. 3–5)

We have several mentions of Priscilla and her husband, Aquila, in the book of Acts and in Paul's letters. We meet them in Acts 18, when they went to Corinth after Emperor Claudius expelled the Jewish people from Rome. There they eventually met Paul during his second missionary journey. As fellow "tentmakers" (Acts 18:3), Priscilla and Aquila became his supporters, companions, and fellow workers in spreading the gospel.

When Paul traveled to Ephesus, he took Priscilla and Aquila with him. Paul stayed in Ephesus only a short time, but this couple remained to become the leaders of a house church in the fourth largest city in the Roman Empire. When Apollos, an influential Jewish Christian from Alexandria, Egypt, passed through Ephesus, Priscilla and Aquila invited him into their home to deepen his understanding of the gospel. When the edict banning Jewish people from Rome was lifted, Priscilla and Aquila returned to Rome to start more house churches.

Priscilla was not the only female leader of a house church. In other letters, Paul mentions Chloe (1 Cor. 1:11) and Nympha (Col 4:15), and in Acts, we meet Lydia, who hosted Paul's missions team and started the house church in Philippi (16:14–15, 40). The names Priscilla and Aquila appear together several times in the New Testament, and most of those instances list Priscilla's name first. Some scholars believe this indicates Priscilla was the primary leader and teacher in the church. It may also speak to her more active role in serving the church.

In Romans 16:3–4, Paul calls Priscilla and Aquila his "co-workers" who risked their lives for his sake and mentions that the gentiles owe them a debt. What an interesting comment to make about their impact on the growing church, indicating they had worked with Paul and influenced how Jews and gentiles worshiped together in the same congregation. Priscilla was, therefore, a prominent church leader who discipled other leaders.

Junia (v. 7)

Right in the middle of Paul's list, we meet Junia and Andronicus. Paul calls them "outstanding among the apostles," which speaks to their comparable level of authority. Junia is the only woman in the New Testament who is called an apostle! This suggests that although we do not read her name in the gospel narratives, she must have been an eyewitness to the life, death, and resurrection of Jesus.

Junia and Andronicus have been believers longer than Paul, and they create enough of a stir in the Roman world to be imprisoned for their faith, right alongside Paul. This is an interesting recognition from Paul that others had effective ministries like his own, traveling throughout the Roman Empire spreading the good news. Junia's ministry went way beyond her household to influence the larger Roman culture.

Live It

Romans 16 is not a common chapter to study, but it is far from a boring list of ancient people we know nothing about. Here we meet our ancient sisters and brothers who did the challenging work of building the church and figuring out how a Jewish message could be received by a gentile audience. There are individuals and families on this list. Males and females. Some who suffered a forced exile from their homes. These names let us know Paul did not go out on his missions alone—he had co-workers and supporters.

This passage also gives us a small window through which to look at the early leadership of the church. We learned of women who led as ministers, apostles, missionaries, preachers, and patrons; at least one was even a prisoner for the gospel. And notice they did not do everything, but in partnership with men served in roles they were well suited for to influence their communities with God's love and salvation through Jesus Christ.

Life Application Questions

1. When you read the descriptions and titles of the women in Romans 16, are there one or two of them in particular whom you easily identify with? Why? Name the women in your life who fulfill some of the same roles as the women in this list.

2. What do you think would change in the church if both men and women understood the types of leadership roles the women of Romans 16 filled?

3. If you're part of a local church, what roles do women play in building up that body of believers? Does it reflect the kind of influence we see the women of Romans 16 had?

4. Paul figures prominently in the New Testament, yet we see in passages like this one that he did not try to do everything by himself. As you think of the variety of roles you play in your life, who has come alongside you as a partner, co-worker, patron, or supporter? How does their support assist you to accomplish your mission?

5. Take a moment to think back over the previous sessions. What new insights do you have about God and how he views women? How can you help younger women recognize their value and potential in God's eyes?

Prayer

God of the enslaved and the free,

God of the leaders, teachers, and witnesses of your character to all people,

God of the women who bear physical or spiritual wounds inflicted due to their gender,

God of people with all skin tones that reflect the different colors radiant in nature,

Remember your daughters today.

Remember those whose talents are ignored because of their gender.

Remember those whom you equipped as leaders, artists, and educators to point others to you.

Remember those to whom you gave a voice but who have been silenced by the church.

Remember those who have given up everything to play a part in your plan of redemption for all people.

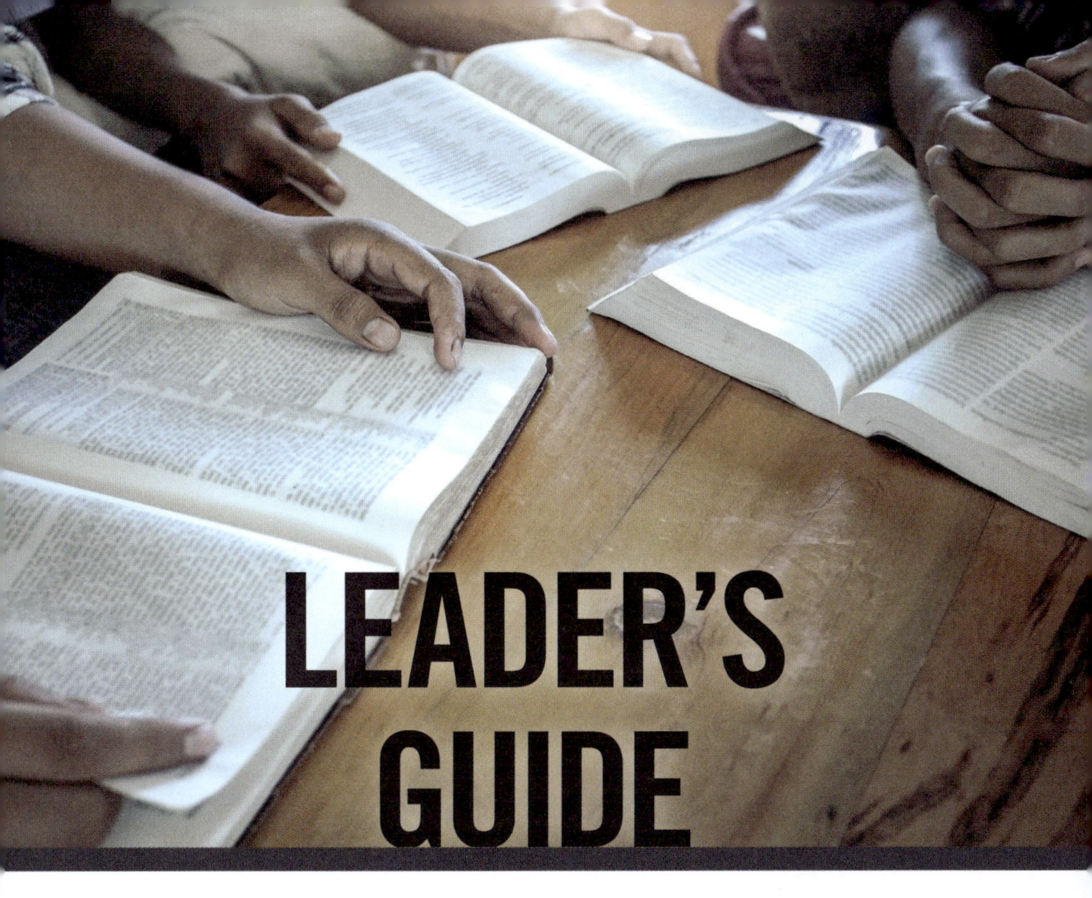

"Encourage one another and build each other up."

1 THESSALONIANS 5:11

Leader's Guide

Congratulations! You've either decided to lead a Bible study, or you're thinking hard about it. Guess what? God does big things through small groups. When his people gather together, open his Word, and invite his Spirit to work, their lives are changed!

Do you feel intimidated yet?

Be comforted by this: even the great apostle Paul felt "in over his head" at times. When he went to Corinth to help people grasp God's truth, he admitted he was overwhelmed: "I came to you in weakness with great fear and trembling" (1 Corinthians 2:3). Later he wondered, "Who is adequate for such a task as this?" (2 Corinthians 2:16 NLT).

Feelings of inadequacy are normal; every leader has them. What's more, they're actually healthy. They keep us dependent on the Lord. It is in our times of greatest weakness that God works most powerfully. The Lord assured Paul, "My grace is sufficient for you, for my power is made perfect in weakness" (2 Corinthians 12:9).

The Goal

What is the goal of a Bible study group? Listen as the apostle Paul speaks to Christians:

- "Oh, my dear children! I feel as if I'm going through labor pains for you again, and they will continue until *Christ is fully developed in your lives*" (Galatians 4:19 NLT, emphasis added).
- "For God knew his people in advance, and he chose them *to become like his Son*" (Romans 8:29 NLT, emphasis added).

Do you see it? God's ultimate goal for us is that we would become like Jesus Christ. This means a Bible study is not about filling our heads with more information. Rather, it is about undergoing transformation. We study and apply God's truth so that it will reshape our hearts and minds, and so that over time, we will become more and more like Jesus.

Paul said, "The purpose of my instruction is that all believers would be filled with love that comes from a pure heart, a clear conscience, and genuine faith" (1 Timothy 1:5 NLT).

This isn't about trying to "master the Bible." No, we're praying that God's Word will master us, and through humble submission to its authority, we'll be changed from the inside out.

Your Role

Many group leaders experience frustration because they confuse their role with God's role. Here's the truth: God alone knows our deep hang-ups and hurts. Only he can save a soul, heal a heart, fix a life. It is God who rescues people from depression, addictions, bitterness, guilt, and shame. We Bible study leaders need to realize that *we can't do any of those things*.

So what can we do? More than we think!

- We can pray.
- We can trust God to work powerfully.
- We can obey the Spirit's promptings.
- We can prepare for group gatherings.
- We can keep showing up faithfully.

With group members:

- We can invite, remind, encourage, and love.
- We can ask good questions and then listen attentively.
- We can gently speak tough truths.
- We can celebrate with those who are happy and weep with those who are sad.
- We can call and text and let them know we've got their back.

But we can never do the things that only the Almighty can do.

- We can't play the Holy Spirit in another person's life.
- We can't be in charge of outcomes.
- We can't force God to work according to our timetables.

And one more important reminder: besides God's role and our role, group members also have a key role to play in this process. If they don't show up, prepare, or open their hearts to God's transforming truth, no life change will take place. We're not called to manipulate or shame, pressure or arm twist. We're not to blame if members don't make progress—and we don't get the credit when they do. We're mere instruments in the hands of God.

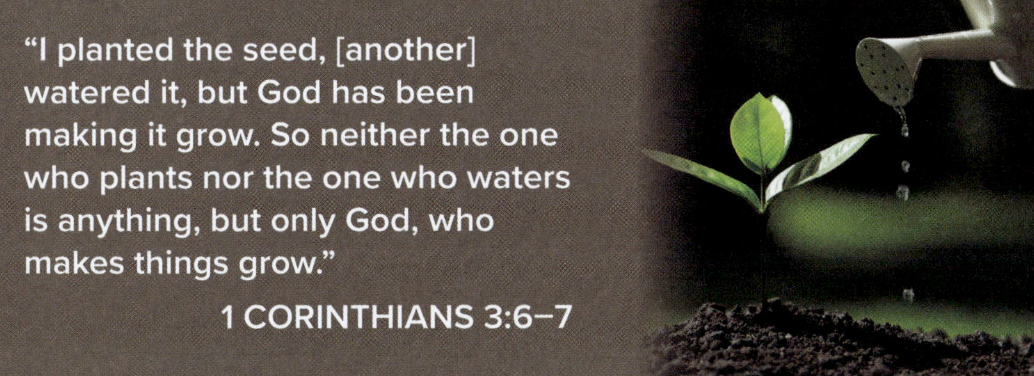

Leader Myths and Truths

Many people assume that a Bible study leader should:

- Be a Bible scholar.
- Be a dynamic communicator.
- Have a big, fancy house to meet in.
- Have it all together—no doubts, bad habits, or struggles.

These are myths—even outright lies of the enemy!

Here's the truth:

- God is looking for humble Bible students, not scholars.
- You're not signing up to give lectures, you're agreeing to facilitate discussions.
- You don't need a palace, just a place where you can have uninterrupted discussions. (Perhaps one of your group members will agree to host your study.)
- Nobody has it all together. We are all in process. We are all seeking to work out "our salvation with fear and trembling" (Philippians 2:12).

As long as your desire is that Jesus be Lord of your life, God will use you!

Some Bad Reasons to Lead a Group

- You want to wow others with your biblical knowledge.

  "Love . . . does not boast, it is not proud" (1 Corinthians 13:4).

- You're seeking a hidden personal gain or profit.

  "We do not peddle the word of God for profit" (2 Corinthians 2:17).

- You want to tell people how wrong they are.

  "Do not condemn" (Luke 6:37).

- You want to fix or rescue people.

  "It is God who works in you to will and to act" (Philippians 2:13).

- You're being pressured to do it.

  "Am I now trying to win the approval of human beings, or of God?" (Galatians 1:10).

A Few Do's

✔ Pray for your group.

Are you praying for your group members regularly? It is the most important thing a leader can do for his or her group.

✔ Ask for help.

If you're new at leading, spend time with an experienced group leader and pick his or her brain.

✔ Encourage members to prepare.

Challenge participants to read the Bible passages and the material in their study guides, and to answer and reflect on the study questions during the week prior to meeting.

✔ Discuss the group guidelines.

Go over important guidelines with your group at the first session, and again as needed if new members join the group in later sessions. See the *Group Guidelines* at the end of this leader's guide.

✔ Share the load.

Don't be a one-person show. Ask for volunteers. Let group members host the meeting, arrange for snacks, plan socials, lead group prayer times, and so forth. The old saying is true: Participants become boosters; spectators become critics.

✔ Be flexible.

If a group member shows up in crisis, it is okay to stop and take time to surround the hurting brother or sister with love. Provide a safe place for sharing. Listen and pray for his or her needs.

✔ Be kind.

Remember, there's a story—often a heart-breaking one—behind every face. This doesn't *excuse* bad or disruptive behavior on the part of group members, but it might *explain* it.

A Few Don'ts

✘ Don't "wing it."

Although these sessions are designed to require minimum preparation, read each one ahead of time. Highlight the questions you feel are especially important for your group to spend time on.

✘ Don't feel ashamed to say, "I don't know."

Disciple means "learner," not "know-it-all."

✘ Don't feel the need to "dump the truck."

You don't have to say everything you know. There is always next week. A little silence during group discussion time, that's fine. Let members wrestle with questions.

✘ Don't put members on the spot.

Invite others to share and pray, but don't pressure them. Give everyone an opportunity to participate. People will open up on their own time as they learn to trust the group.

✘ Don't go down "rabbit trails."

Be careful not to let one person dominate the time or for the discussion to go down the gossip road. At the same time, don't short-circuit those occasions when the Holy Spirit is working in your group members' lives and therefore they *need* to share a lot.

✘ Don't feel pressure to cover every question.

Better to have a robust discussion of four questions than a superficial conversation of ten.

✘ Don't go long.

Encourage good discussion, but don't be afraid to "rope 'em back in" when needed. Start and end on time. If you do this from the beginning, you'll avoid the tendency of group members to arrive later and later as the season goes on.

How to Use This Study Guide

Many group members have busy lives—dealing with long work hours, childcare, and a host of other obligations. These sessions are designed to be as simple and straightforward as possible to fit into a busy schedule. Nevertheless, encourage group members to set aside some time during the week (even if it's only a little) to pray, read the key Bible passage, and respond to questions in this study guide. This will make the group discussion and experience much more rewarding for everyone.

Each session contains four parts.

Read It

The *Key Bible Passage* is the portion of Scripture everyone should read during the week before the group meeting. The group can read it together at the beginning of the session as well.

The *Optional Reading* is for those who want to dig deeper and read lengthier Bible passages on their own during the week.

Know It

This section encourages participants to reflect on the Bible passage they've just read. Here, the goal is to interact with the biblical text and grasp what it says. (We'll get into practical application later.)

Explore It

Here group members can find background information with charts and visuals to help them understand the Bible passage and the topic more deeply. They'll move beyond the text itself and see how it connects to other parts of Scripture and the historical and cultural context.

Live It

Finally, participants will examine how God's Word connects to their lives. There are application questions for group discussion or personal reflection, practical ideas to apply what they've learned from God's Word, and a closing thought and/or prayer. (Remember, you don't have to cover all the questions or everything in this section during group time. Focus on what's most important for your group.)

Celebrate!

Here's an idea: Have a plan for celebrating your time together after the last session of this Bible study. Do something special after your gathering time, or plan a separate celebration for another time and place. Maybe someone in your group has the gift of hospitality—let them use their gifting and organize the celebration.

	30-MINUTE SESSION	60-MINUTE SESSION
READ IT	Open in prayer and read the *Key Bible Passage.* 5 minutes	Open in prayer and read the *Key Bible Passage.* 5 minutes
KNOW IT	Ask: "What stood out to you from this Bible passage?" 5 minutes	Ask: "What stood out to you from this Bible passage?" 5 minutes
EXPLORE IT	Encourage group members to read this section on their own, but don't spend group time on it. Move on to the life application questions.	Ask: "What did you find new or helpful in the *Explore It* section? What do you still have questions about?" 10 minutes
LIVE IT	Members voluntarily share their answers to 3 or 4 of the life application questions. 15 minutes	Members voluntarily share their answers to the life application questions. 25 minutes
PRAYER & CLOSING	Conclude with a brief prayer. 5 minutes	Share prayer requests and praise reports. Encourage the group to pray for each other in the coming week. Conclude with a brief prayer. 15 minutes

	90-MINUTE SESSION
	Open in prayer and read the *Key Bible Passage.* 5 minutes
	• Ask: "What stood out to you from this Bible passage?" • Then go over the *Know It* questions as a group. 10 minutes
	• Ask: "What did you find new or helpful in the *Explore It* section? What do you still have questions about?" • Here, the leader can add information found while preparing for the session. • If there are questions or a worksheet in this section, go over those as a group. 20 minutes
	• Members voluntarily share their answers to the life application questions. • Wrap up this time with a closing thought or suggestions for how to put into practice in the coming week what was just learned from God's Word. 30 minutes
	• Share prayer requests and praise reports. • Members voluntarily pray during group time about the requests and praises shared. • Encourage the group to pray for each other in the coming week. 25 minutes

Group Guidelines

This group is about discovering God's truth, supporting each other, and finding growth in our new life in Christ. To reach these goals, a group needs a few simple guidelines that everyone should follow for the group to stay healthy and for trust to develop.

1. **Everyone agrees to make group time a priority.**
   We understand that there are work, health, and family issues that come up. So if there is an emergency or schedule conflict that cannot be avoided, be sure to let someone know that you can't make it that week. This may seem like a small thing, but it makes a big difference to your other group members.

2. **What is said in the group stays in the group.**
   Accept it now: we are going to share some personal things. Therefore, the group must be a safe and confidential place to share.

3. **Don't be judgmental, even if you strongly disagree.**
   Listen first, and contribute your perspective only as needed. Remember, you don't fully know someone else's story. Take this advice from James: "Be quick to listen, slow to speak, and slow to become angry" (James 1:19).

4. **Be patient with one another.**
   We are all in process, and some of us are hurting and struggling more than others. Don't expect bad habits or attitudes to disappear overnight.

5. **Everyone participates.**
   It may take time to learn how to share, but as you develop a trust toward the other group members, take the chance.

If you struggle in any of these areas, ask God's help for growth, and ask the group to help hold you accountable. Remember, you're all growing together.

Notes

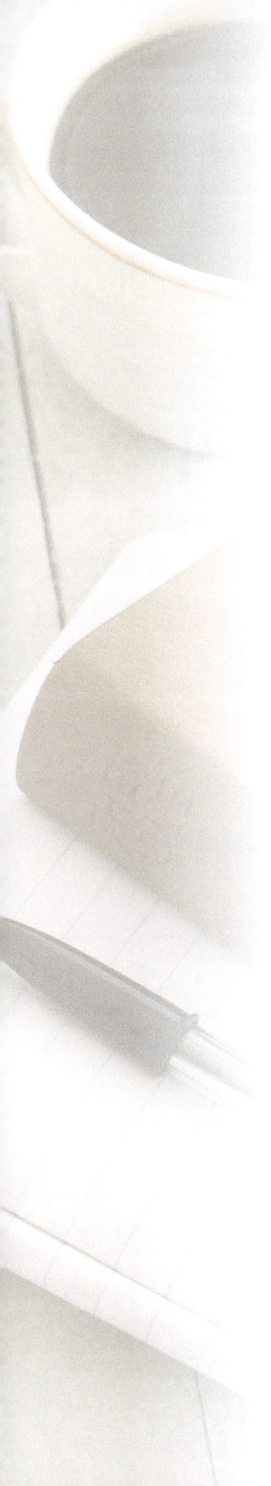

ROSE VISUAL BIBLE STUDIES

6-Session Study Guides for Personal or Group Use

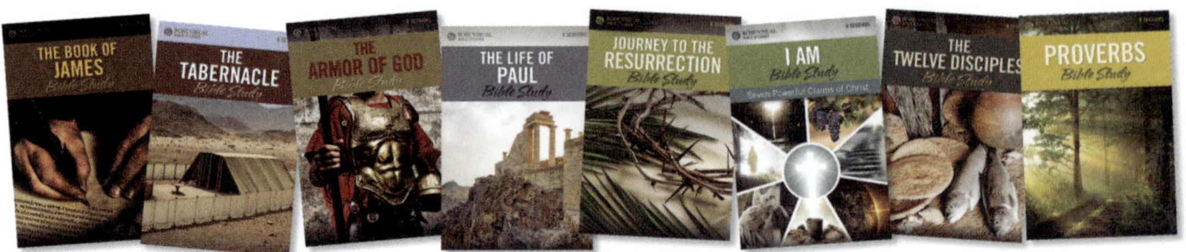

THE BOOK OF JAMES
Find out how to cultivate a living faith through six tests of faith.

THE TABERNACLE
Discover how each item of the tabernacle foreshadowed Jesus.

THE ARMOR OF GOD
Dig deep into Ephesians 6 and learn the meaning of each piece of the armor.

THE LIFE OF PAUL
See how the apostle Paul persevered through trials and proclaimed the gospel.

JOURNEY TO THE RESURRECTION
Renew your heart and mind as you engage in spiritual practices. Perfect for Easter.

I AM
Know the seven powerful claims of Christ from the gospel of John.

THE TWELVE DISCIPLES
Learn about the twelve men Jesus chose to be his disciples.

PROVERBS
Gain practical, godly wisdom from the book of Proverbs.

WOMEN OF THE BIBLE: OLD TESTAMENT
Journey through six inspiring stories of women of courage and wisdom.

WOMEN OF THE BIBLE: NEW TESTAMENT
See women's impact in the ministry of Jesus and the early church.

THE LORD'S PRAYER
Deepen your prayer life with the seven petitions in the Lord's Prayer.

FRUIT OF THE SPIRIT
Explore the nine spiritual fruits.

PSALMS
Discover the wild beauty of praise.

THE EXODUS
Witness God's mighty acts in the exodus.

THE BOOK OF JOB
Explore questions about faith and suffering.